RAISING KIDS TO
EXTRAORDINARY
FAITH

RAISING KIDS TO EXTRAORDINARY FAITH

HELPING PARENTS & TEACHERS DISCIPLE THE NEXT GENERATION

DEBBIE SALTER GOODWIN

BEACON HILL PRESS
OF KANSAS CITY

Copyright 2008
by Debbie Salter Goodwin and Beacon Hill Press of Kansas City

ISBN 978-0-8341-2391-5

Printed in the
United States of America

Cover Design: J.R. Caines
Interior Design: Sharon Page

Library of Congress Cataloging-in-Publication Data

Goodwin, Debbie Salter.
    Raising kids to extraordinary faith : helping parents and teachers disciple the next generation / Debbie Salter Goodwin.
        p. cm.
    Includes bibliographical references (p.   ).
    ISBN 978-0-8341-2391-5 (pbk.)
    1. Child rearing—Religious aspects—Christianity. 2. Christian children—Religious life. 3. Discipling (Christianity) I. Title.

    BV4529.G662 2008
    248.8'45—dc22

                                                            2008038872

10 9 8 7 6 5 4 3 2 1

To Mark, my husband and partner in love, in life, and in Christ, who has helped me make discipleship a priority in parenting and ministry.

CONTENTS

ACKNOWLEDGMENTS

Although this book was not my idea, it grew in my heart as if it were. I especially want to thank Lynda Boardman, Director of Children's Ministries for the International Church of the Nazarene, who gave me the opportunity to write this. Her passion for this project encouraged me from the beginning. I'm also indebted to her staff for reviewing ideas, drafts, sharing resources, and perspectives. I'm especially grateful for Beula Postlewait, Children's Ministries International Coordinator. Thank you for your support, quick responses, and productive suggestions.

An integral part of the research for this book was a survey that went out to parents and ministry workers. I appreciate the work of Ken Crow and the Research Center of the Church of the Nazarene for sending the surveys and compiling the results. Your contribution was a jumpstart in my process. And to those of you who filled out the surveys, my heartfelt thanks for your candid and helpful responses. The theme that ran through each one was a hunger to be a part of a parent-church partnership that makes the spiritual lives of our children a non-negotiable priority.

Thanks to Beacon Hill Press of Kansas City Director Bonnie Perry and her remarkable staff, whose commitment to quality and whose kindness to me make any partnership in publishing a joy.

Special thanks to Mark, my husband, my sounding board, first editor, and faithful affirmer. I'm always better at anything because of you.

To those who discipled me, my parents, Sunday School teachers, Caravan leaders, and a long list of faithful Christians whose lives I watched, thank you for your part in introducing me to the joy of following Jesus. I'm truly the sum of many parts.

RAISING KIDS TO
EXTRAORDINARY
FAITH

INTRODUCTION

How can we help children become lifelong disciples of Jesus?

How can we utilize the partnership potential between home and church?

How can we help children become independent learners as disciples of Jesus?

These are the questions that fueled the writing of this book. From the beginning it has been about linking parents and ministry workers in the instruction Jesus left to make disciples. To obey the Great Commission, we must include the children.

Discipling is more than Christian parenting. In Christian parenting, the parent is the Christian. Discipleship focuses on a child who has made a profession of faith. It becomes a day-by-day, experience-by-experience adventure.

Discipling is more than teaching about being a disciple. The danger of a book about discipling children is that someone will think it's about transferring information and skills. That would allow anyone who has the right information to pass it on and check off discipling.

But discipling is about sharing with others the model of the life you live in Christ. It engages them in the adventure of following Jesus.

While discipling children begins in the home, it's important to support it in every component of the family of God. Life is the learning lab, and every Christian has influence in the lives of children.

So who should read this book? Anyone who wants to be a part of a support circle to grow a young disciple. That goes beyond parents and ministry workers. It includes extended family and friends. It includes every person in the community of faith where children are present. We all have to be ready to share our lives, our faith stories, and our encouraging words to help children follow Jesus.

A 13-week Leader's Guide is available as a free downloadable resource at <www.beaconhillbooks.com>. It offers parents and teachers an opportunity to come together, learn together, and plan together to make discipleship the first priority in ministry to children. Use it as an elective for parents, as a training resource, or as a small-group study. Since partnership is a key theme, find a way to partner as you study.

For some, the first few chapters may seem overwhelming. For others, this book doesn't go far enough. To all, this is a beginning. My prayer is that this book will bring together parents, pastors, ministry workers, and educators to take another step toward the partnership that will make a difference in the lives of our children. We *can* raise children who are transformed by extraordinary faith. We *can* raise lifelong disciples of Jesus who understand early that salvation gives them a life beyond what they could ask or dream. We *can* disciple the next generation.

Let's do it together!

Discipleship is the current
that keeps the bird in flight.
—*Emily, children's pastor*

1
WHERE DISCIPLE-MAKING BEGINS

Go . . . make disciples.
—MATTHEW 28:19

They walked in, anonymously mixing with the Temple crowd. What was so special about one more couple bringing their baby for the commanded visit? Mary and Joseph were probably just as nervous as you were your first time out in public with a newborn. Still learning about the cries and needs of the baby who had changed every routine of their lives, they were no doubt more focused on the baby than anything else.

They had been taught about the importance of this visit. They had witnessed other parents making this first family trip to God's house. Now it was their turn. Pride tumbled with wonder. Joy wrestled with fear. They were to raise this child for God. The only way to begin was with obedience.

Christian parents need to do more than raise good kids who go to church. They need to raise disciples.

The timeless truth about this visit is that it would have been the same no matter who the baby or parents were. It reminds us that God believes in families. It tells us that if Jesus' parents needed to keep this appointment with God's command, we can do no less.

For Christians, parenting is about more than just raising good kids. It's about raising *God's* children *God's* way. It's about keeping trust with God and His Word. From the beginning of time, God demonstrated His belief that the family is the best place to learn about Him and how to live in His world.

While good parenting skills and church involvement are critical, they are not a substitute for godly nurture and teaching at home. Christian parents need to do more than raise good kids who go to church. They need to raise disciples who want to follow Jesus as long as they live.

Discipleship isn't something you can add to life like a special trip. Discipleship *becomes* the life of any follower of Jesus. To raise a generation of disciples who will continue to change their world with the transforming message of the gospel requires parents and others who themselves are making this same commitment.

Today's parents are the ones who grew up
in the church with specialized ministries
for every age group. The church has sold
itself as [the place] to meet all your
needs. In return, parents don't know or
think to realize that *they* are the forming
center in a child's life and the church is a
supporting beam in the process.

—Cindi, pastor of family life

The story of Legion in the New Testament demonstrates the importance Jesus places on home and family. Legion was the lunatic who lived in the caves. The transforming call of Jesus sent his demons packing and gave Legion his right mind back. Legion understood this as nothing short of a miracle. Of course, he wanted to follow the Miracle Worker. He was ready to get in the boat and leave everything, just as the Twelve who traveled with Jesus had done.

"Go home to your family and tell them how much the Lord has done for you, and how he has had mercy on you" (Mark 5:19).

Parents don't have to guess where their disciple-making mission takes place. It's at home with their children. Home should be where children expect to hear the salvation stories of their parents. It should be the place where words about God and the actions and attitudes of our lives deliver the same message. Home is where we learn how to be disciple-makers.

Talking with your children about spirituality is like talking about sexuality: many want to do it but don't know how.

—*Bruce, father of three*

However, God doesn't dump this discipleship responsibility into the lap of parents without support. Nor does He want a child without Christian parents to be like the seed that dies for lack of a nurturing context. He expects the faith community to be an integral part of discipling His children. God knows that it will take more than parents and extended family to raise a lifelong follower of Christ. It will take every pastor, every teacher, and every volunteer who intersects a child's life. It will take a focused, consistent, and ongoing approach from every Christian who has influence with children. No one is exempt in the discipling process.

When Jesus delivered His last verbal instructions before His ascension, He said, "Make disciples" (Matthew 28:19). It wasn't a suggestion for us to vote on or an idea to consider. Jesus had already given His life for this one-on-one approach. He empowered the Eleven with His plan for making disciples: "Teach these new disciples to obey all the commands I have given you" (Matthew 28:20, NLT).

Think about children as fledgling followers. Think about their eagerness for adventure, their innocent trust, their boundless energy. Think about channeling everything that childhood offers with the goal of growing disciples. What would happen if innocent trust keeps growing? What would happen if energy fuels mission? What would happen if the adventure of following Jesus never waned? They would not only change their world—they would change ours as well.

All followers of Jesus receive the same instructions—parents, friends, family, ministry volunteers, and pastoral staff. Anyone who touches a child's life is on call for Jesus to use as a disciple-maker.

> **Anyone who touches a child's life is on call for Jesus to use as a disciple-maker.**

However, it takes a disciple to make a disciple. It takes those who have made following Jesus a daily commitment to lead someone else along the same road. That's where it gets up-close and personal. That's where those who work with children must examine their own lives as disciples and ask some serious questions:

- What happens if children follow Jesus in the same way I do?
- Am I willing to be transparent about my own journey as a disciple of Jesus?
- Where do I substitute knowledge for relationship?

A DISCIPLE IS . . .

Let's start with a definition easy enough for a child to understand: A disciple is someone who follows Jesus, loves Jesus, learns from Jesus, and obeys Jesus in all of life. Discipleship is a relationship with Jesus that's based on love, guided by His commandments, and nurtured in a community of faith. Discipleship is both a decision about life and the life itself.

For parents, this definition is a reminder of their accountability to Jesus as the real parental authority in a child's life. Parents need more than their best ideas to raise disciples. They need to know that Jesus leads them as they parent His children. It means everything sends them back to God and His Word— sibling rivalry, leisure boundaries, scheduling priorities, discipline—it's all about discipling.

What Parents Say

- Find teachable moments each day to model what it means to be a follower of Jesus.

  —*Kati, mother of two*

- Our primary responsibility as parents is to pass on our faith to our children.

  —*Belinda, mother of two*

- I know this is my responsibility, but I'm often unsure of how I'm doing.

  —*DaVonne, mother of nine*

- I feel like I have the knowledge, I have the support; I just don't have whatever it takes to make important things a priority over urgent things that demand my attention.

  —*Michele, parent*

- I think for most parents communicating with their children on a spiritual level can be intimidating.

  —*Betty, mother of four*

What Ministry Workers Say

- Discipleship is not ideas and resources—it's a lifestyle that needs to be modeled.

  —Cindi, pastor of family life

- As children's ministry workers, we're only the "surrogates."

  —Tammy, ministry worker

- Parents need to see their own need for discipleship, no matter how long they've been a part of the Church.

- Wise is the mom or dad who lives out Christ 24/7 in front of his or her kids.

  —Jerry, children's ministry consultant

For teachers and others who invest in children's lives, the definition gives the real reason for their involvement in the life of a child. They must answer the question "How does my involvement in this child's life grow a disciple?" They can't allow themselves to get sidetracked by teaching information or rules to the exclusion of modeling what a disciple looks like, talks like, thinks like, acts like, and loves like.

Disciple-making doesn't happen by accident. It isn't caught by reading Bible stories together. It isn't just a set of skills or answering Bible questions correctly, and it certainly isn't just about faithful church attendance. Discipleship is a matter of the heart and will, mind and soul, body and spirit. There's nothing that a person says, thinks, dreams, or does that doesn't come under the discipleship umbrella.

WHAT DOES THIS MEAN FOR YOU?

No matter what your relationship to a child is, there's a discipling role for you to play. Sometimes it's impromptu. Sometimes it's planned. Sometimes you're the primary discipler. Sometimes you're support. It's body life in action.

Take a look at the following components of disciple-making. How are you doing with the children within your circle of influence?

Live a daily commitment to Jesus. First of all, a disciple keeps his or her life as a follower of Jesus up to date. Every day is an opportunity to apply fresh insights about how following Jesus makes a difference in relationships, in contentment, in goal-setting, in everything. It's when we connect these life lessons to the Scripture and principles we want children to understand that it begins to turn light bulbs on for them.

Model what it means to follow Jesus. Nothing substitutes for a flesh-and-blood example, because children are literal and concrete. They don't apply ideas as easily as they follow examples. God understands that we all learn that way. That's why God brought Jesus to us in the flesh—because ideas and instructions aren't enough. We must also commit ourselves to show and not just tell how to live as a disciple. We must be honest about how discipleship shows up in our television and movie choices. We must be honest about how it governs our decisions about money and time. We can't offer them our best idea about being a disciple—we have to offer them our *journey*.

Tell the story. The story God wants us to share is about a love that never goes away. It's about how God spared nothing to rescue us from our own destructive self-centeredness. Tell the story to children as many times as you can. Use pictures and activities and books. No other story has the potential to give children their most valuable gift—eternal life.

Spend one-on-one time. At some point, discipling is a one-on-one model. You can successfully teach the big principles, the great stories, and the basic skills in groups with activities. But group discipling will always fall short. It's the one-on-one process that encourages questions, gives uniquely shaped encouragement, and provides personal accountability. For parents, this can take place in the car, during a meal, before bedtime, and in a number of impromptu moments that open up each day. For ministry volunteers, this might mean time before class, a scheduled time outside of class, a personal exchange in an unplanned encounter. Not every teacher may be able to make a one-on-one commitment with each child, but every child should have more than a parent committing one-on-one time.

Read and discuss God's Word together. There's no substitute for God's Word. It must have a central place in the home and classroom. Home issues should make you search the Scriptures for God's principles. Classroom questions should do the same. If our children never see us answer their questions by searching God's Word, how can we expect them to make their own personal discoveries?

Help children become disciple-makers. When anyone decides to follow Jesus as His disciple, he or she also joins the disciple-making mission of God's plan. As parents and ministry workers, we must help children understand this component of being a disciple.

Pray together. Discipling children takes more than praying *for* them. It takes praying *with* them. There are many opportunities throughout a family's day when this can happen. Other disciple-makers must also look for opportunities. Don't simply tell a child that you'll pray *for* him or her. Pray *with* the child first.

Encourage questions. Let children's questions tell you what they're ready to learn. From simple curiosity to critical inquiry, questions open doors to personal learning and application. Don't expect to have all the answers. Sometimes their questions make you a learner with them in a way that bonds all of you as disciples in the making.

Celebrate growth. We celebrate good grades, soccer game wins, birthdays, and any number of accomplishments in the lives of our children. How do we celebrate a decision to follow Christ with equal enthusiasm? How do we celebrate when a child rejects temptation or applies something from God's Word to life? This is a fun way to support a child on a discipleship journey. Perhaps when we start celebrating discipleship milestones in the same way we celebrate other events, children will get the message—discipleship rocks!

TIME TO GET SERIOUS

It's time for all of us to stop passing the buck. Parents want the church to do a better job teaching children about following Jesus. The church wants the home to do a better job. The truth is that by working together, we'll all do a better job raising disciples for the next generation.

We have the most exciting adventure ahead of us. And the statistics are in our favor. Early training does make a difference. Godly models do matter. While there's no guaranteed formula for instant results, we can have the confidence of knowing that there's nothing God wants more than for us to help Him get His children home.

Will it take new ideas? Probably. Will it take a wisdom that doesn't come from books? Absolutely. Most of all, it will require that each of us takes himself or herself to the Master Disciple-maker. As we present ourselves to Jesus, ask for His empowerment, and obey His instructions, we'll become the disciples our children need.

There's nothing God wants more than for us to help Him get His children home.

FOR PARENTS

1. Where have I expected the church to be responsible for my children's discipleship?

2. What will happen if my children reproduce the way I follow Jesus?

3. When can I plan a special time to share my salvation story with my children.

4. Where do I need to take following Jesus more seriously?

FOR MINISTRY WORKERS

1. Where have I taught lessons about following Jesus without sharing my journey?

2. Who needs one-on-one discipleship time from me?

3. What demonstrates my commitment to discipling children?

4. What can I do differently as a disciple-maker this week as I intersect the lives of children?

A DISCIPLE-MAKER'S PRAYER

Loving God, if following you helps others follow you—especially children—then help me follow more closely, obey more completely, and share my journey more specifically.—An earnest follower

2
HEARING
JESUS
CALL

"Come, follow me," Jesus said.
—MATTHEW 4:19

"Trevor!" his mother called out the back door. It was just seconds before Trevor answered by running toward the voice he knew belonged to his mother. Whatever he had been doing took second place to presenting his whole self before his mother.

Of course, children don't always answer parents immediately. Nor do they drop everything to make answering a full-body focus. But when they do, what takes place?

- They recognize who called.
- They understand how answering benefits them.
- They demonstrate a desire to answer.
- They stop anything that does not help them answer.

We all know that sometimes children answer parents out of duty or just to stay out of trouble. Neither produces positive results. Growth-producing maturity occurs as they learn the importance of answering a parent's call quickly.

How does a child hear and recognize the invitation of Jesus? Look at the story of God calling Samuel. When Samuel was a boy, God called him, but Samuel at first didn't recognize who had called him. He didn't expect anyone except Eli to interrupt his sleep and ask for his attention. Samuel responded the way he was prepared to respond—he checked in with Eli.

So what did Eli do when Samuel came to answer him? He sent him away because he hadn't called him. Obedient Samuel went back to bed—but not for long. Once again he heard the call. Without hesitation, Samuel went back to Eli. But Eli still hadn't called him and sent the boy to his sleeping mat again. Then it happened a third time—and that's when Eli woke up to what was really going on.

Here's what's interesting and what's also an important lesson to all of us. Eli didn't spend a lot of time explaining what had happened. He simply told Samuel how to respond, instructing him to answer with the words "Speak, Lord, for your servant is listening" (1 Samuel 3:9). When Samuel followed this instruction, a whole new relationship began between a boy and his God, one that influenced and shaped the rest of his life.

That's what we want for our children, isn't it? Early listening, early responding. However, it doesn't happen in a vacuum. It isn't an automatic response to church attendance or Sunday School. Since answering Jesus' invitation to follow Him requires a response of the heart, it will take heart-deep teaching, modeling, and nurturing on several levels to prepare our children to hear, recognize, and answer the invitation of Jesus. How do we do that?

TELL THE STORY

Parents should be the first to share the salvation story with their children. Then, ministry workers have the opportunity to build on a child's understanding of what it means to live the story. That's where the partnership between home and church is important. If you're a parent, ask for the resources and training that will help you. If you're a ministry worker, look for creative ways to supply them.

Find as many ways as you can to tell the story of Jesus and His gift of salvation to us. Purchase special Bible storybooks that tell the Christmas and Easter stories. No one outgrows the beautifully illustrated versions of these timeless stories. Make sharing God's salvation plan a key part of your family's Christmas and Easter celebrations. Do the same in the classes you teach. Continue to share how God's gift of salvation turned your life around.

The free downloadable leader's guide for "My Best Friend, Jesus"[1] offers a model for a simple and complete gospel presen-

Creative Ways to Tell the Christmas Story

- Turn rooms in your house into places from the Christmas story (Herod's palace, the road to Bethlehem, the field, the stable). Place appropriate costume pieces and/or props in each. Move from room to room, telling the story as children use costumes and props.

- One mother turned her unused outbuilding into a stable and told the Christmas story to extended family, most of whom had not made a profession of faith in Christ.

- Unpack a Nativity set as the first Christmas decoration. Choose places in different parts of the house for Mary and Joseph, shepherds, and Wise Men. Each day move different figures closer to the stable as you talk about the story.

- Wrap the baby Jesus figurine from a Nativity set and put it under the Christmas tree to be opened first thing on Christmas morning. Then read the Christmas story.

tation. It helps you tell the story of Jesus in a focused way to explain God's plan of salvation.

How many times do children need to hear the salvation story before they respond to Jesus' invitation? There's no magic number. However, if we're intentional in our families and ministry assignments to share God's salvation story, we increase the probability that at some point the child will be ready.

In 1 Peter 3:15 we're reminded, "Always be prepared to give an answer to everyone who asks you to give the reason for the hope that you have." That isn't just an admonition for ministry workers. It involves parents too. Be ready with a list of key verses. Be ready with a simple way to share God's plan of salvation. You don't have to be a theologian or someone with the spiritual gift of evangelism. If you're continuing to be transformed because of your decision to follow Jesus and have a positive connection with a child, you're the best person to share the story.

HOW EARLY CAN A CHILD BELIEVE?

I've seen in my years of ministry that the parents who spend the most time talking to their children about Christ and are good role models to their children have children who are ready to make a decision at a younger age.

—Maryanne, preschool ministry

Just how early can a child really believe? There are as many answers to this question as there are children. Perhaps talking about an "age" is misleading. It's more like a stage. While the elementary years may be the expected time, there are children who respond to Jesus earlier or later.

Children will respond to Jesus' invitation with the same developmental ability they exhibit in other areas of their lives. Following Jesus doesn't help a child mature faster. Rather, following Jesus shapes the maturing process. The principle is to

---

God's Plan of Salvation

God is all love and wants to have a loving friendship with you. (See 1 John 4:16.)

Sin breaks our friendship with God. (See Romans 3:23.)

God loved us so much that He sent Jesus, His Son, to take care of our sin problem. (See 1 John 4:9.)

Jesus willingly paid the punishment for our sin by dying on a cross. (See Romans 5:8.)

God raised Jesus to life so that anyone who believes in what Jesus did can have God's life too. (See Acts 5:30 and Romans 3:23.)

---

nurture an age-appropriate understanding and response. Very young children respond to the love of Jesus, older preschoolers begin to connect loving Jesus with loving actions, while elementary children can experience spiritual remorse over sin and respond to Jesus' forgiveness. It's critical that parents and teachers look for the signs in a child's life that he or she is getting ready to answer an invitation from Jesus.

HOW DO YOU KNOW WHEN A CHILD IS READY?

There's no litmus test we can apply to determine when a child is ready to follow Jesus. Jesus deals with each child based on personality, experience, knowledge, and abilities. However, there are signs we can look for.

Pay attention to their questions. Children's questions tell us a lot about what they're thinking. Questions about baptism, Communion, and heaven can easily lead you to speak with a child about following Jesus.

Pay attention to their answers. Children's answers come

from the way they perceive the world. While adults find many of their perceptions humorous, they can understand a lot about what children understand by identifying the source of answers that don't line up with facts and truth. That's especially true with a child's understanding of God. Ask questions to find out why a child thinks the way he or she does. In the process, you may realize that a child is thinking more about God and spiritual matters than you expected.

Be alert to their interest in spiritual matters. Look for ways children initiate conversations and questions about spiritual matters. If a child wants to apply a Bible lesson to life without adult cueing, that's a sure sign that Jesus is making His invitation known to that child. Be an Eli, and help the child understand how to respond to Jesus. When children start making personal connections between their lives and Jesus' gift, they're very close to making it a personal story.

Respond to fears about their spiritual lives. A child's immature grasp of his or her world may put things together in ways that produce fear. The knowledge that someone is always watching may not be a comforting thought to a child until it is balanced with the perfect love of Jesus. While Jesus doesn't use fear to get a child's attention, we must listen for fear as a sign that a child wants a security that only responding to Jesus can give.

Be sensitive to their discomfort or rejection of spiritual matters. Sometimes children fight against what they really want, because they fear it could never be true for them. Look for the source of this discomfort. Talk about how different the disciples were when Jesus invited them to follow Him. Point out that Jesus knows each of us by unique personality and asks us to do only what He knows we can accomplish.

THE ABC PLAN OF SALVATION

When a child is ready to say yes to Jesus, it's important to guide the child through a simple process to emphasize the life-changing components. "Simple" is best for children. The ABC plan has a three-word outline: Admit, Believe, and Claim. The free downloadable leader's guide for "My Best Friend, Jesus"[1] also shares this as a way to guide a child's prayer to become a follower of Jesus.

A is for _Admit_. Tell God you've disobeyed Him. (See Romans 3:23.)

B is for _Believe_. Believe God loves you and sent His Son, Jesus, to make it possible for you to be forgiven. Ask for and receive God's forgiveness. (See John 3:16.)

C is for _Claim_. Claim Jesus as your Savior and best friend. "Claim" means to know for sure that Jesus is _your_ Savior. Begin to live as a child of God. (See Romans 10:13.)

STARTING THE JOURNEY

Now the fun begins! There really isn't anything more exciting than to help a new believer explore the adventure of following Jesus. Be ready with the "So . . . You Want to Follow Jesus?" packet.[2] It's a simple, interactive Bible study that addresses the key elements of new life in Christ. Immediately teach a child how God's Word now becomes a map for life. Learning what God's Word says and means will become a motivating and exciting quest. Remind a child that prayer is our moment-by-moment lifeline to God. God is always listening and ready to share anything that will help us live this new life. Chapter 3 shares ways that the family, ministry workers, and the community of faith can celebrate and affirm the decision a child makes to follow Jesus. Chapters 5 and 6 talk specifically about prayer and Bible study.

Meet with the children's ministry workers to pray together about a child's decision to become a follower of Jesus. Make this an ongoing relationship of accountability and support.

JUST ASK

Don't be surprised if children find it easier to hear Jesus' invitation than we expect. Four-year-old Thomas asked his father why Jesus died on the Cross. This was the day Thomas's parents had prayed for ever since they knew he would be born. With love and simplicity, the dad retold the Easter story. Then he asked if Thomas wanted to ask Jesus into his heart. Thomas looked up at his dad and said, "I already did." Stunned, his dad asked when this happened. With the nonchalance that only a child shares, Thomas said, "When I was playing today."

While his father accepted what Thomas said, inside he doubted that a four-year-old could make such discovery. Later, God reminded the dad that it was not his place to determine what Thomas understood about a decision to follow Jesus. It was his responsibility to help Thomas learn what it meant.

Remember: Jesus values childlikeness. He lifts their innocence and simple trust up as examples for adults to emulate. These are the characteristics that help children hear and respond to Jesus' invitation early. Accept their decision to follow Jesus even when it seems to come from incomplete understanding. That's the way that Jesus accepts them. Let their understanding about what it means to be disciples of Jesus grow at a similar rate to their physical, mental, and emotional development.

What a precious moment when a child
makes the connection to understand what
Jesus has done for him or her!

—*Mary Beth, ministry worker*

MAKING A PERSONAL DECISION

Answering an invitation to follow Jesus is always individual and personal. While parents and teachers may influence the process, we cannot manufacture the response. It wasn't enough for Andrew to bring his brother Simon to Jesus or for Philip to bring Nathaniel. Simon and Nathaniel had to respond to the implications of Jesus' invitation for themselves.

For us, that means that we can bring our children to Jesus, but unless they answer *His* invitation, they won't become disciples. They must be able to recognize the voice of Jesus, give attention to that voice, and respond with actions that place them within the teaching circle of Jesus. They must engage in an ongoing relationship marked by one-on-one communication between a fledgling disciple and the Master disciple-maker. If as parents or teachers we set up situations in which a child depends only on what we say about Jesus, we grow children who don't expect to learn directly from Jesus. They may expect Jesus to lead parents and teachers, pastors and missionaries, but they may not understand that they can stand shoulder-to-shoulder in that same group and hear Jesus' words of invitation and direction to them.

LIFELONG FOLLOWING

Listening for the call of Jesus isn't just for beginning the relationship with Jesus as a disciple. It's a lifelong skill. What better time than childhood to begin a discipleship journey that's all about listening and responding to what Jesus says? Whether it takes a WWJD (What Would Jesus Do?) reminder bracelet or daily conversations in the family, the foundational activity of discipleship begins and continues with listening to Jesus. How can you as parent or teacher encourage a child to follow Jesus daily?

- Make sure following Jesus is *your* priority before talking to a child about how it should be his or her priority.

- Ask questions that require listening to Jesus to find an answer.

- Memorize scripture so that Jesus can use scripture as reminders.

- Ask children to share times when Jesus reminded them of a scripture.

- Build confidence that Jesus will communicate if we listen.

- Share ways that listening to Jesus helps you follow Him.

Jesus called the crowd to him and said,

"Listen and understand."

—Matthew 15:10

39

IF THEY DON'T HEAR ABOUT JESUS AT HOME

Many children in church come from homes where listening and following Jesus aren't a priority. Make sure that a child understands that it's not a choice between listening to Jesus and listening to parents. Listening to Jesus will help a child be more loving and obedient to parents. This is important for children to understand.

Look for special ways to support these children. Spend one-on-one time with them to earn the right to ask questions about spiritual matters. Since no one at home asks what they think about God and His story, plan to find ways to ask the questions you wish parents were asking. When a child exhibits spiritual sensitivity, consider matching the child with a mentor who will follow up weekly and be available for questions and extra support. Join the child in praying for the parents. Help the child realize what it means to be loved into the family of God.

He who has ears, let him hear.

—Matthew 11:15

BE AN ELI IN A CHILD'S LIFE.

Every child needs an Eli who looks for signs that Jesus is calling a child. Be there to encourage a Samuel response when a child hears Jesus share His invitation to follow Him. Be there to explain the next steps. Be there to celebrate new understandings and growth. Whether it's as parent or ministry worker, we become coworkers with God in His mission to get His children home. We become disciple-makers. We influence the eternal destiny of children.

FOR PARENTS

1. How can you demonstrate to your child that you expect Jesus to invite him or her to follow Him?

2. How did you recognize and respond to the invitation of Jesus in your life as a child?

3. How could you plan to tell the Christmas and Easter story in a special way this year?

4. Are you prepared with a simple outline and scriptures to help your child make a personal decision to follow Jesus?

FOR MINISTRY WORKERS

1. Have you shared with children how Jesus called you to be His disciple? If not, when could you?

2. What is your plan for presenting the salvation story to the children in your ministry assignment?

3. How can you be an Eli in the life of a child?

A DISCIPLE-MAKER'S PRAYER

Ever-present God, I want to be ready to share your story with children in a way that makes them want to follow you for the rest of their lives. Help me.

3
AFFIRMING FAITH

Now that faith has come.
—GALATIANS 3:25

When Jacob told his parents that he had made a decision to follow Jesus during children's worship, his parents were ecstatic. They wanted him to call his grandparents. They talked about it during lunch. They wanted to take him out for ice cream. There were extra hugs and a special prayer his father prayed. *Wow!* Jacob thought. *This is a bigger deal than I realized.*

How we respond to a child's decision to follow Jesus is extremely important. It sets a pattern for how we'll treat other spiritual decisions. Children take their cues from the significant adults in their lives. Although there are exceptions, children usually value what the influential adults in their lives value. As parents and teachers, we're the key influencers. How should we value and affirm a child's decision to follow Jesus? How do we communicate God's desire for it to be a lifelong choice that requires daily commitment? How do we initiate a process that helps a child learn what it means to live as a follower of Jesus? We all have work to do to celebrate and nurture this decision.

TO AFFIRM

To *affirm* is to make a specific declaration of intent. It is to validate, confirm, and dedicate ourselves toward a specific purpose. When a child makes the declaration to live under the rule and tutoring of Jesus, the immediate family and the extended family of Christ have an opportunity to acknowledge this decision and support it. The celebration needs to have a life-changing feel to it that communicates to the child how big the circle of support is. It needs to open the door to an adventure— learning how to live the decision to follow Christ.

CELEBRATE NEW DECISIONS

Everybody loves a celebration. We celebrate birthdays, anniversaries, graduations, sport victories, first days, last days. We're always looking for an excuse to get people together for a special reason. However, as we review the list of what we generally celebrate, where are the parties for spiritual victories? Jesus himself taught us that "There is rejoicing in the presence of the angels of God over one sinner who repents" (Luke 15:10). If a decision to follow Jesus is a good-enough reason for a celebration in heaven, shouldn't we do the same? Besides, what better way to affirm a child's decision than with a celebration? Children understand what it means to celebrate.

CELEBRATE AS A CHRISTIAN FAMILY.

Next to entering the physical world as an air-breathing human being, birth into spiritual life in Christ is just as world-changing. Make it just as important.

- Record the date in a special place, like a family Bible.
- Call the family together for a special prayer.
- Create your own memory certificate, and post it in the child's room as a visual reminder.
- Invite friends and family for a spiritual birth celebration. Ask celebrants to bring a scripture to include in a memory book. Consider sharing other family salvation stories at this occasion.
- Give a gift to honor the decision. It could be anything from a new Bible to something symbolic.
- Celebrate this spiritual birthday every year as a time to evaluate spiritual growth and set new goals for the year to come.

CELEBRATE AS A COMMUNITY OF FAITH

The church family also needs to find its place in celebrating new faith decisions, especially with children. There are as many ways to do this as there are congregations. Find the way that works for your congregation. Review your plan often, especially when key leadership changes.

Whether you're a parent or ministry worker, share the child's decision with key ministry staff. Find a way to help the child make a public testimony. It could be as simple as working with your pastor to invite the child and family to come to the altar at prayer time. It could also include lighting a salvation candle while sharing the name of the child who has made a new decision for Christ. Sometimes interviewing a child about his or her new decision is appropriate. Ministry leaders should encourage adult believers to find their own way to support the child in this new journey. Some may write a note; others may share their congratulations in person. There's great accountability in making public a personal decision to follow Jesus. The early disciples were very public about their commitment as disciples of Jesus. We need to help children do the same.

SPREAD THE NEWS

The stories of Jesus' disciples remind us that someone was always telling someone else about Jesus. Encourage the child to call someone who has been praying for this decision in the child's life. It could be a grandparent, aunt, Sunday School teacher, or other family friend. Talk about how to tell friends at school. Explain how to use opportunities that demonstrate the changes that following Jesus initiates. These can involve language, attitude, showing more compassion, and a number of other factors.

Help children understand that sometimes their friends notice a change because of what a person does. Sometimes they notice a change because of what a person does *not* do. Initiate conversations with the child about how Jesus can empower a new follower to use these opportunities as a way to share His good news with others. Encourage your new believer to tell someone and just keep increasing the circle. Jesus' last instruction on earth to all of us was to make disciples. The best time to make this a part of following Jesus is immediately following a new decision.

Christian parents have the best opportunity to affirm a child's new faith in Christ. A child's decision to follow Christ creates another relationship bond within a blood family. It's not simply genetics or marriage that creates the family circle. It's the blood of Christ and His sacrifice. Child and parent are united in an eternal way. Because of that new relationship tie, it should affect family relationships in positive ways.

First, it creates opportunities for spiritual conversations in the family. These are informal ways to talk about life in Christ. They need to be the norm within a Christian family. It's more than "What did you learn in Sunday School?" It involves asking how Jesus made His presence known throughout the day. The more conversations you have with your child about his or her relationship with Jesus, the more focused you can be about your discipleship responsibility.

It also changes the way a family prays together and individually. Christian parents need to pray more after a child makes a decision for Christ, not less. The journey has just begun. Pray each day that the child understands something new about Jesus. Pray that he or she understands how to trust God, obey Him, and never stop learning about Him. Make sure it's not a one-sided prayer opportunity. Ask your child to pray for you about a concern. This models the importance you place on prayer and the child's relationship to God. Remember: Jesus asked His disciples to pray for Him. It was a significant part of His disciple-making. It must be part of ours as well.

Make each day an opportunity for the family to learn something about who God is and how life with Him is better than life without Him. This will help children grow in their relationship with Him. It requires that parents be at least one step ahead of a child's spiritual journey. That has less to do with knowledge and more to do with spiritual sensitivity and transformation. As God transforms your life because of your trust and obedience, let it spill over into the lives of your children. This is discipleship at its best!

AFFIRM WITH FOLLOW-UP

We don't abandon newborns to their own devices to find the best way to grow up, nor should we abandon children who have made decisions to follow Jesus. They need one-on-one help. There are several ways to make this happen.

- Make sure the child has a discipleship partner. This is a prayer partner, an encourager, a mentor. Even if parents fulfill this role first, it's helpful for children to have at least one other one-on-one supporter.

- Use "So . . . You Want to Follow Jesus?"[1] This is a five-week Bible study packet to help a child understand the key foundations for new faith. Ministry workers can use it in a small-group setting. Parents can use it informally at home.

- Be careful not to overwhelm a child in the early stages of living out this decision. Remember that the Holy Spirit is the child's primary guide. Ask more questions than you give information so that you can cooperate with and build on a child's understanding.

- Make sure the child has a Bible version that fits his or her understanding and reading ability. Chapter 6 talks about selecting a Bible for each learning and maturing stage.
- Ask your pastor when the next baptism class is, and talk to the child about participating.
- Encourage the child to talk to God every day just as he or she talks to a friend. See chapter 5 for more ideas about teaching children to pray.
- Talk about the importance of taking the Bible seriously as the most important way to find out how God wants His children to think, talk, feel, and act. See chapter 6 for ways to teach a child to study the Bible.

More Ideas for Parents

- Set a regular time to work with your child through the Bible study from "So . . . You Want to Follow Jesus?"

- Set a regular time to pray with and for your child about specific concerns.

- Encourage older children to work with younger siblings to develop their disciple-making skills.

More Ideas for Ministry Workers

- Develop e-mail or postal encouragement notes to send to new believers.

- Consider a follow-up plan that involves the whole family, especially in situations where the child does not have Christian support at home.

- Present an age-appropriate Bible to the child.

Make sure that your process to affirm a new decision in Christ allows the child to explain what he or she understands. Never assume anything; always ask questions. "What does this decision mean to you?" "Why did you make this decision now?" Then build on whatever understanding the child has. For example, even if a child makes a decision for Christ because others were doing it, use it as an opportunity to help the child know the importance of turning that group decision into a personal decision.

The Book of Acts reminds us of how diligent the apostles were in nurturing new Christians. They visited towns even when it endangered their lives. They wrote letters to encourage, confront, and disciple. Today we have phones, e-mail, mail service, and multiple church gatherings that we can use for discipleship training. However, one-on-one personal discipleship builds relationships for accountability.

Summer camp has always been a highlight for me to see children come to know Jesus. I follow up camp with a membership class and Bible study and have children experience a Celebration of Faith service that includes Communion, baptism, prayer, and healing.

—Gerald, discipleship pastor

LET THE SACRAMENTS AFFIRM

Children respond to the visual message that baptism presents. They begin to understand the public confession involved in following Jesus. They like the idea of celebrating their decision in a special way. That's the gift of sacraments. They show—they don't just tell. Of course, we need to prepare children to understand what the sacraments demonstrate. We need to explain that a sacrament is an action Jesus instructed us to repeat. It shows an outside picture of what God does on the inside. We need to talk about them as object lessons or visual aids to teach us about God's gift of grace.

Protestants recognize two sacraments: baptism and Communion. Parents and ministry workers have innumerable opportunities to use these sacraments to help children understand and affirm what God wants to do in their lives. The ideal scenario occurs when parents help children understand the meaning and purpose for the sacraments, and ministry workers provide the occasions to worship and celebrate through the sacraments. How do parents prepare for these important opportunities?

The easiest way is to take children to services of baptism and Communion and be ready to answer their questions. Write down any questions you're unable to answer, and consult with your pastor. Always follow up with the child to answer his or her questions.

Make sure that you connect involvement in the sacraments as a way to affirm a decision to follow Jesus. Consider attending a baptism class or a church membership class with your child as a way to process the information together, even if your child is not ready to participate in baptism or membership. Use the pamphlets "So . . . You Want to Be Baptized?"[2] and "So . . . You Want to Take Communion?"[3] Check out the ideas and activities included in the downloadable leader's guide for each. Share the information the child is ready to process and apply. Let the child's questions help you know what that is.

Be personal in the way you talk about the sacraments. Explain how they remind you of God's gift of salvation. Talk about how you use them to review before God your decision to follow Jesus. Encourage curiosity with reverence. For example, most children are very curious about the place where people are baptized. There's nothing wrong with addressing that curiosity with a visit to the baptistery with a staff minister.

A time when the community of faith celebrates one of the sacraments can be followed with focused conversation about it. Ask questions such as "Do you understand what it meant?" "Did you notice how special it was?" Help children to understand that celebrating the sacraments are God-filled moments. A child who understands them in this way uses the sacraments as a continuing affirmation of faith.

Baptism

The most important way to affirm new faith is with Christian baptism. Jesus is very clear about the place this represents in a person's life-turning. In fact, no other confirmation is more crucial to the person and the family of God than the celebration of Christian baptism. Don't overlook the immense possibilities here in the discipling process.

Baptism by immersion demonstrates what happens when we confess our faith in Jesus. A new believer goes under the water, paralleling what happened when Jesus died and was

---

Teaching Discipleship Through the Sacraments

- Explain the meaning of baptism and Communion.
- Use the "So . . . You Want to Be Baptized?" and "So . . . You Want to Take Communion?" pamphlets and downloadable leader's guides.
- Make sure children attend services that include baptism and Communion.
- Answer children's questions.
- Encourage reverent curiosity.
- Pray that children understand the spiritual story behind the sacraments.
- When a child prays to become a follower of Jesus, invite him or her to celebrate the decision with baptism and Communion.

---

buried. Then the believer comes out of the water, raised to the new life God gives. Water, a familiar cleansing agent, represents the cleansing only God's work can do. (See Colossians 2:12.) Words just can't explain conversion in the same way.

Don't underestimate the power of the baptism class as a key opportunity to present the gospel in a way that children can understand. The very meaning reenacts the salvation story. That's why it's important to invite children who show sensitivity or even curiosity to the invitation of Christ. Invite children to attend with at least one parent. That allows parents to reinforce the information at home.

It's important that the time between a child's affirmation of faith and baptism be a relatively short period. Some suggest that there be no more than three to five weeks between the de-

> One new second-grade girl listened intently during the children's sermon and said to me, "Ms. Becki, it seems to me that when John the Baptist baptized all those people and then Jesus, that—well, Ms. Becki, do people who follow God all get baptized to show they believe that Jesus is God's Son?" When I assured her that they do, she gushed, "Ms. Becki, you're going to have to find a way to get me baptized!"
>
> *—Becki, ministry worker*

cision to follow Jesus and baptism. This may require the pastoral staff to rethink the way they plan baptism services. Churches that do not have easy access to a baptistery may need to consider ways for a child to make a public affirmation until the next baptism service.

Make sure the church family celebrates baptism together. Prepare special invitations that a child can hand out to friends and relatives. You might be surprised at how many will come to support a child for this special event. Plan a way for family and friends to gather and congratulate the child. Make it easy for the family of God to celebrate decisions to follow Christ.

If we're not careful to teach a child to know Christ, he or she will grow up thinking that being a Christian is nothing more than a magic aisle, a magic prayer, or a magic dunking booth.

—Reagan, children's pastor

Communion Affirms

The first time a child participates in the Lord's Supper should be a very special time for the family and the community of faith. Make sure the pastor and key children's workers know that the child is participating as a follower of Jesus for the first time. If you're the parent, give your child an opportunity to share what it meant to him or her to take Communion with the rest of the family. Celebrate it in a special way. Pray a special blessing over the child who participates in Communion for the first time.

Ministry workers can encourage children to share with other children why Communion is special to them. Acknowledge a first Communion, and connect it to the decision to follow Jesus. Invite a child who does not have Christian support at home to sit with you. Or recruit a family who will "adopt" a child. Encourage other children in the family to model the meaning of Communion. Don't underestimate the role of children in reaching out to other children. Besides, this is a critical part of learning to be a disciple-maker.

THE CHRISTIAN CALENDAR

One way to help children see their lives in light of God's gift of salvation is to celebrate the Christian calendar. This involves more than remembering what God did at Christmas and Easter. It includes ways to celebrate the preceding weeks and those that follow these pivotal points in Christian history. While there are several versions of the Christian calendar,[4] here is a simple listing of some of the most basic seasons:

Advent: The four weeks leading to Christmas provide an opportunity to prepare for the spiritual message of God's gift. Using an Advent wreath, candles, special devotionals, and family activities will keep the real message of Christmas a priority in your family and the church.

Christmas: The anniversary of the birth of Jesus is packed with family traditions. Make sure it contains just as many activities to focus on why Jesus' birth is so important. At church, help children move past commercialization. Acknowledge festivities and excitement, but focus on the spiritual foundations of Christmas.

Epiphany: Also called Three Kings' Day, the 12 days following Christmas recall the time when the Eastern magi came to worship Jesus. This time celebrates God's desire to include the whole world in His plan for salvation. This is a good time to make family plans for a personal mission thrust within your neighborhood, extended family, city, or other world areas. Since some children may be absent from church during the Christmas holidays, this allows you to extend the celebration of Jesus' birth.

Ordinary Days or Ordinary Time: "Ordinary" comes from *ordinal,* as in numbers to count. This is the time following Epiphany until Lent and following Pentecost until Advent. Use these days to focus on different aspects of discipleship or the stories of Jesus.

Lent: These 40 weekdays lead up to Good Friday and end on the Saturday before Easter. It's a time to think carefully about what Jesus did for us. Many do without a pleasure or food item to emphasize Jesus' sacrifice.

Holy Week: This is the week before Easter. It's a time to review Jesus' last week. It begins with Palm Sunday and also includes Maundy Thursday and Good Friday.

Easter: This is the Sunday that God resurrected Jesus from the dead and is the pivotal point of the Christian calendar. Again, this day has many secular and family components. Evaluate your celebration at home and church based on how it helps your children know the real meaning of Easter.

Pentecost: 50 days following Easter, this is the Sunday that celebrates the gift of the Holy Spirit. Review what it means to live by the power of the Holy Spirit in your family and at church.

Ordinary Days or Ordinary Time: As explained above, this is the counted days until Advent and is a good time to review the teachings of Jesus.

For more ideas about how to use the Christian calendar in your family or classroom, check out the downloadable 13-week leader's guide for this book, or research ideas on your own.

We put so many events on our calendars—why not start marking our calendars with reminders that keep us focused on what God has done for us? When our children understand that the life of Jesus is something we talk about and celebrate daily at home as well as in church, they can't help but see how following Jesus is the warp and weft of life. It's a critical component in creating a context that encourages a child to make a lifelong decision to follow Jesus.

AN AFFIRMING YES!

There are few opportunities in ministry as rewarding as becoming a part of a discipleship process that affirms a child starting a lifelong journey to follow Christ. We say to that child: "Yes, we agree with the decision you have made. Yes, we're on the same journey. Yes, we want you to go with us."

God's affirmation to us is that we can live every day of our lives in relationship with Him. Teaching children to hear and enjoy God's affirmation is an exciting process. Just think—if children live God's affirmation every day of their lives, return to it during difficult times, and share His affirmation with their friends, what kind of people of faith will they become? How will they change this world?

Let's find out.

FOR PARENTS

1. How have you celebrated your child's decision to follow Jesus? What are some ways you would like to celebrate this?

2. What place does baptism play in the affirmation of your faith? How have you or how will you communicate that with your child?

3. Who besides you is helping to disciple your child? Have conversations with anyone filling that role, and update each other on the progress you see.

4. How could you use the Christian calendar as a part of your family tradition?

FOR MINISTRY WORKERS

1. Do you know what your church's plan is for celebrating new decisions for Christ? Have you and other ministry workers incorporated this plan in ministry assignments?

2. Do you know how your church identifies candidates for baptism? Is there a component that makes it easy for children to learn about and participate in baptism?

3. Do you work with children who do not have discipleship support at home? How can you create a plan that gives them the support they need?

4. What plan do you have or need to make to follow up with children who make new decisions to follow Jesus?

A DISCIPLE-MAKER'S PRAYER

Affirming God, help me live your affirmation so that the children in my circle of influence will be hungry to receive and apply your affirmation to their lives.—Celebrating my life in you!

4
FOLLOWING
TO
OBEY

If you love me, you will obey what I command.
—JOHN 14:15

When Jesus called His disciples, there wasn't much discussion about the invitation. He called their names and invited them to follow Him. In every situation, the men took it as a total life change. They left fishing boats, families, shelter, and money. Following Jesus changed everything they did every day. Whatever Jesus said, they did. They followed His instructions about their first independent mission trip. (See Luke 9:3-6, 10.) They went ahead when He gave them instructions about planning for Passover. (See Luke 19:29.) And when Jesus told them to wait in Jerusalem until they received the Holy Spirit, they waited. (See Luke 24:49.) The longer they followed Him, the more they understood the importance of obedience. Obeying Jesus always took them to the right person or the right action.

Obedience is the unmistakable characteristic of a disciple of Jesus. It is not something up for debate at each turn of the journey. The decision to follow Jesus *is* a decision to obey Him.

Children must understand this and anchor the early stages of their discipleship in obedience. Obeying Jesus is where growth happens. It's important that they connect obedience to a relationship of love. Without love, obedience is duty. With love, obedience is a privilege that results in more than would be possible without it.

There are 169 occurrences of some form of the word "obey" in the Old Testament and 62 occurrences in the New Testament, depending on the translation you use. Twelve of the New Testament occurrences are direct quotes from Jesus. There is no substitute for obedience, no way to follow Jesus without obeying Him.

TEACHING OBEDIENCE

Teaching children to obey is one of the first important tasks of parenting and discipleship. It doesn't take long before we realize that children aren't born to obey. They may be complacent or easygoing in ways that make them more cooperative.

However, the desire to obey parents, teachers, rules, and boundaries is not automatic.

The same is true of a child's new journey of faith. A decision to follow Jesus must be backed up by a life of obedience. Obedience puts the teeth in a decision to follow Jesus. Obedience grows extraordinary faith. It's the mustard seed miracle. Plant obedience; grow faith.

However, we're not referring to just any kind of obedience such as obedience in order merely to please or to keep out of trouble. Rather, it's obedience that comes from growing trust in the one you obey. In the case of making Christlike disciples, it's growing trust in the character of Jesus.

Ask children who they want to grow up to be like, and they'll name someone they respect or look up to. Who do they want to learn more about? Usually it's someone who's bigger than life to them. Who will they follow no matter what? Someone who won't let them down. Our discipleship responsibility is to make sure that children know they can answer those questions with Jesus.

Our first assignment in growing young disciples to obey Jesus is to teach them who Jesus is. We must help them fall in love with a God who pulled out all the stops to make a difference in their lives by sending His Son, Jesus. We must give them countless experiences to know firsthand that Jesus can be trusted more than anyone else they know.

Here's the tricky part: we can't do it just through Bible stories. Children must have some "life lab experiments," some opportunities to find out why obedience is always a choice and why it doesn't happen automatically. They also need opportunities to find out what happens when they don't obey Jesus. They need to learn how to connect obeying Jesus with what they read from His Word.

Again, the most important influencers in this process are parents. They're the ones with day-to-day contact. They're the ones who have more teachable moments. They're the ones who can take an immediate life experience and transform it into a moment of spiritual growth and understanding. However, all ministry workers can help children learn that attitudes and choices affect every area of life, including the spiritual.

MORE THAN GOOD PARENTING

Nothing has challenged my Christian growth more than parenthood. The responsibility to represent Jesus to my daughter is overwhelming. It makes me desperate for the kind of spiritual growth in my own life that makes it easier to be accountable to God for my parenting practices. Early on I came to understand that Christian parenting is not just about my best idea or even some authoritative person's best idea. Christian parenting is about keeping my surrender to God's wisdom up to date. Christian parenting is about staying close enough to God so that I hear His whisper about when to speak and when to remain silent. Christian parenting is simply an outgrowth of *my* obedience to God. My personal obedience equips me to teach the life of obedience to my child.

Why do you think God put families together in the first place? It wasn't so that you had something special to celebrate on Mother's Day and Father's Day. It was to raise more people to know and follow God. Mass evangelism and missionary work were backup plans to spread the message to those who did not learn it as children. It's a responsibility, a challenge, and a part of our own obedience to God that we can't ignore. When we don't disciple our children, we make it necessary for someone else to fill the gap.

OBEDIENCE BEGINS AT HOME

If we want children to learn to obey Jesus, we begin by teaching them to obey their parents. The verses that emphasize the importance of children obeying parents make it clear how God feels about it:

- "Children, obey your parents in the Lord, for this is right" (Ephesians 6:1).

- "Children, obey your parents in everything, for this pleases the Lord" (Colossians 3:20).

God is a God of order. He knows that our homes become places of order when there's obedience. That's why He sets it up as a standard for family living. However, it must be obedience connected to God-given authority for the physical, emotional, and spiritual good of His children. The discipleship opportunities within the responsibility of parents are enormous. Obedience teaches self-discipline, perseverance, authority, submission, and acting for the greater good while reducing selfishness and insensitivity. Parents who don't know how to teach their children to obey will struggle to help their children learn how to obey Jesus.

When children have been taught to obey their parents as their first earthly authority, it's easier to learn to obey God as their ultimate and eternal authority. Check out information about age-appropriate readiness as you set your expectations in this area. Early success is important.

Ten Commandments for Children

1. Keep God in first place in everything.
2. Don't let anyone or anything become more important than God.
3. Treat God's name as special.
4. Treat God's day as special.
5. Respect and obey your parents.
6. Protect life.
7. Protect faithfulness in marriage.
8. Don't steal.
9. Don't lie.
10. Be content with what you have.

START WITH GOD'S WORD

God does not expect us to guess about the starting place for obedience. He has given us His Word. Any discussion about obedience must include the Bible. Every story, lesson, letter, reminder, and warning in God's Word gives us plenty to obey.

God summarized the starting point for obedience in the Ten Commandments. Post them in your home or classroom. Personalize them. Talk about how the commandments apply to television, DVDs, games, movies, sports, school, family—every part of life. Talk about how they protect the life and dignity of everything God created. Talk about obeying God's request that He be your first priority because it's the best way to keep the other nine commandments.

THE HEART OF OBEDIENCE

Obedience in the life of a disciple of Jesus is much more

than behavior modification. Obedience includes the will, motive, and intent as well as actions and thoughts. In the life of a young disciple it's not just about following some rule, even though it may start there. Rather, it's about allowing the character of Jesus to help a young believer trust that whatever Jesus says will be for his or her best. How do you do that?

1. Lead with the love of Jesus for your child. It's easy to help young children believe that Jesus loves them. Their innocence gives no reason to doubt this love. As children grow up, they question more as they experience hurt, disappointment, and unavoidable grief. It's even more critical to maintain an image of Jesus' love in all these circumstances. Help children realize that whatever hurts a child grieves Jesus. Review the stories in which Jesus used children as an object lesson to teach all of us how He values children.

Help children look for ways Jesus communicates His love in difficult circumstances. When something doesn't go the way a child expected, take time to pray about it as a family or class. Have specific conversations about it. Ask, "How is Jesus trying to let you know how much He loves you in the middle of this?" Make it an ongoing conversation in your family or class.

When a child, or anyone else for that matter, perceives love from another, obedience is not a burden—it's a privilege. It becomes the way to enrich and deepen a relationship. Let love lead any discussion about obeying Jesus.

2. Connect obedience to loving Jesus. Always speak about obeying Jesus as a way to love Him. That's what Jesus taught His disciples: "If you love me, you will obey what I command" (John 14:15). If there's an obedience problem, look for something your child doesn't understand about the love Jesus has for him or her. It might be the fear of not getting what he or she wants. It might be immaturity about connecting love and obedience. Does the child really understand that Jesus knows best? What is there about your life experience that models to a child that obeying Jesus is always better than anybody's best idea?

3. Share simple ways to obey together. It's always more fun together. Pray about this as a family or class. What does Jesus want *us* to do? This is not just brainstorming for good ideas. This is about receiving a specific assignment. Be sensitive to the innocent leading of children. Sometimes they put us to shame with their openness to obeying Jesus outside their comfort zones. Families should take the opportunity to pray about obedience in sports involvement, vacations, and leisure choices—everything that affects family life. Ministry workers can also do this at church. Everyone can learn important lessons about the increased confidence that comes from obeying together.

As a parent or teacher, when you share a Bible story or lesson with children, do you look for what Jesus wants you to obey from the lesson first? When the lesson gives you something to obey, your teaching has a depth and life relatedness that involves more than creative teaching ideas.

4. Make sure children understand that a decision to follow Jesus is a decision to obey. How can anyone decide to follow Jesus without obeying Him? If there's even a possibility to choose whether to obey or not, is it really a decision to follow Jesus? Help children understand that a disciple never tries to decide if there will be obedience. The only appropriate questions are *when* to obey and *how*.

5. Talk about growing the desire to obey. It's not about

All of Life—All Obedience

Obedience Involves—
Our Minds

"Love the Lord your God with . . . all your mind" (Matthew 22:37).

"Then he opened their minds so they could understand the Scriptures" (Luke 24:45).

Our Wills

"Eagerly desire the greater gifts" (1 Corinthians 12:31).

"As obedient children, do not conform to the evil desires" (1 Peter 1:14).

Our Bodies

"Offer your bodies as living sacrifices, holy and pleasing to God" (Romans 12:1).

"Do you not know that your bodies are members of Christ himself?" (1 Corinthians 6:15).

Our Resources

"Do not store up for yourselves treasures on earth, where moth and rust destroy, and where thieves break in and steal" (Matthew 6:19).

"Share with God's people who are in need" (Romans 12:13).

Our Hearts

"It is with your heart that you believe and are justified" (Romans 10:10).

"Whatever you do, work at it with all your heart, as working for the Lord" (Colossians 3:23).

Our Future

"I know that his command leads to eternal life" (John 12:50).

"Live lives worthy of God, who calls you into his kingdom" (1 Thessalonians 2:12).

What do you do that doesn't fall into one of these categories?

perfect obedience—it's about developing the *desire* for obedience. When the heart of a child connects to the heart of Jesus, it's that loving connection that grows obedience. Without that connection, obedience can be reduced to duty. Duty will never grow a disciple. Only God through His Holy Spirit can do this heart-shaping work. A parent, teacher, or other influencer in a child's life can testify to God's work in his or her own heart and model what happens when a person lets the desire to obey grow. However, the real work belongs to God and the child. We can't make a child obey, but we can pray that the desire to obey grows.

6. Share how obedience makes things happen that will occur no other way. It's important to talk about your own journey of obedience. Tell about a time you were obedient to Jesus by reaching out to someone you would not have thought of on your own. How did an obedient action influence the direction of a circumstance that was poised to go wrong? Help a child understand that Jesus doesn't want us to obey Him out of a desire for control—He wants us to obey Him because He sees and knows everything about the circumstances we face. He knows what will make the biggest difference. His Word shares the basics. Then, as we practice more and more obedience, we begin to learn how He directs with specific details that bring about realizing His will.

RESPONDING TO TEMPTATION

Another important component of learning to follow Jesus has to do with learning to recognize and confront temptation. The second lesson taught in "So . . . You Want to Follow Jesus?" reminds us that a "temptation is anything that makes us want to disobey God." The Bible says that temptation will be a part of our lives. As parents and children's workers, we know that sometimes it's difficult to understand what represents a true temptation to a child and what belongs to a natural maturity process. One important difference is that a temptation stands in the way of pleasing God. On the other hand, an immature child may have the desire without the physical, mental, or emotional ability to carry through. This is very important to recognize when working with children who have learning and other emotional or mental delays. A child with ADHD can't just try harder. He or she must try different ways to overcome unhelpful or inappropriate behavior.

A temptation is anything that makes

us want to disobey God.

—"So . . . You Want to Follow Jesus?"

What surfaces as a temptation to a child may seem rather insignificant to us. As spiritual mentors in the lives of children, we need to take the temptations they face very seriously. What they learn about facing temptation will follow them for a very long time.

WHAT THE BIBLE SAYS ABOUT TEMPTATION

Always talk to a child about temptation using a clear foundation from God's Word. This is Bible training 101. What does the Bible teach? The best summary comes from 1 Corinthians 10:13:

Everyone faces temptation.

God will not allow a temptation you can't overcome.

God provides a way through temptation.

Rejecting temptation makes you stronger.

Other scriptures add the following:

God is not the author of temptation. (See James 1:13.)

Prayer helps us confront temptation. (See Matthew 26:41.)

Jesus experienced and overcame temptation. (See Luke 4:1-13.)

Children have to be taught how to grow in the Lord so they can handle the choices they have to make when they're with their peers.

—Mike, children's pastor

Explain the difference between feeling tempted and giving in to temptation. Illustrations are as numerous as children's circumstances. Something someone said makes a child angry and registers a desire to lash out verbally or physically. Make sure the child understands that *feeling* as if you want to do something wrong is the temptation. It becomes a problem only when you give in. Sometimes the temptation is to act without thinking. The reflex to make a hurtful comment is giving in to the temptation to act what you *feel* without considering what pleases Jesus.

Help the child understand that temptation is an attack using a desire or weakness. (See James 1:14.) When a fighter wants to win in the ring, he or she looks for a weakness or place of vulnerability. Satan, our tempter, does the same thing. He's an underhanded enemy out to win by any means. He makes our desire look reasonable. That's the way he conned Eve into eating the forbidden fruit.

Help children know that God understands their weaknesses. He wants to give His strength to protect us from letting weakness become a place of spiritual failure. Tell children to think of a weakness as a special place for God to show His strength. It's a critical step in spiritual growth.

Children need to understand that there are God-pleasing ways to fulfill God-given desires. For example, a boy can want the $20 bill he saw his friend drop. To take money he knows is not his is the wrong way to fulfill the desire. To look for ways to earn money is a good way to fulfill the desire.

Acknowledge how difficult it is to confront temptation. While the temptations a child faces may not seem as difficult to overcome as temptations you face as an adult, they're just as challenging. The difficulty comes in what we attach value to. Fighting the temptation to go along with an inappropriate activity with your friends is just as difficult as saying no to the urge to cheat on income tax.

EQUIP CHILDREN WITH TEMPTATION-BUSTERS.

There are many ways to overcome temptation. Have regular

conversations about ideas that children could use best. Here are some examples:

- **Arrow prayers.** These are quick "Help me" prayers to God. Focusing on getting help from God is the first way to confront temptation. This is more helpful than focusing on what to do with a person or a circumstance.

- **Apply scripture.** Memorize 1 Corinthians 10:13 as a family or class. Talk about the good news that God will not allow anything to come into your life that you can't say no to. Celebrate the truth that God will always show you how to confront temptation without giving in to it. Share how overcoming temptation makes you stronger. Make sure these conversations are linked to real-life experiences. Don't just talk about how it's possible to identify and confront temptation—talk about what happened when you did.

- **Feel remorse.** Remind children that remorse or sadness about what you did or didn't do is God's way of getting your attention so He can help. Don't try to *make* a child feel bad. That's shame, and God does not shame a person. God's Word reminds us that "Godly sorrow brings repentance" (2 Corinthians 7:10).

- **Talk to someone.** Talking about a specific temptation is one way to face temptation. It takes away the secrecy and builds accountability. Be the person a child can talk to about any temptation. Be God's representative to express to the child that God never stops loving a person, even when he or she gives in to temptation. Explain that God is more than ready to help a child learn how he or she could respond to temptation differently another time.

Helping Children Overcome Temptation
How parents can support

Share a symbol to remind your child that you're praying. It could be a bracelet, necklace, card, token, or just a colored dot placed conspicuously on a watch-band.

Write a prayer, and include it in lunch, book bag, or purse. Send a text message if your child has access to a cell phone. Make sure the child can access it without disobeying school policy.

How ministry workers can support

Share a "call me" card. Offer to listen or pray any way and at any time.

Prepare "temptation-buster" cards to pass out. These are a set of pocket-sized cards. One side has a temptation-buster idea from above, and the other side lists a scripture.

Keep a list of scriptures about temptation handy.

- **Just say no.** The easiest time to say no to temptation is the first time you recognize it. The longer you think about it, the harder it gets. Sometimes we say no to inside ideas that tempt us to do or say the wrong thing. Sometimes we say no to people who want us to do or say the wrong thing. No matter what the temptation is, the bottom-line answer is no. The shorter the time between the temptation and saying no, the greater the growth.

WHEN A CHILD GIVES IN

How do you respond to a child who gives in to temptation? With great love and acceptance, especially when he or she is honest about it. Review the opportunities for a different choice. Find out if the problem is about impulse. Try to uncover a fear that took control. Don't just talk about it—pray about it. Let the child pray and express his or her feelings and intent. As a representative of God, speak specific words of God's acceptance as a pronouncement of blessing over the child. This is the priestly work of parent or ministry worker. This is an opportunity to stand with a child in a difficult but redeeming moment. It's your opportunity to place the hand of the child into the hand of God and then step out of the way.

A PROVING GROUND

Overcoming temptation is difficult also because temptation usually comes without warning. There's no time to prepare for it. That's why it's important to teach children to do the preparing all along. Don't overwhelm children with information about how to deal with temptation later in life. Children live in the literal present. They need to know what makes a difference right now. Give them "right-now" answers.

Temptation is the proving ground for discipleship. Every time a disciple turns away from temptation, he or she is stronger. It's like a pop quiz. Temptation gives a disciple the opportunity to put into practice what he or she is learning about following Jesus.

Be sure to celebrate any victory over temptation. Family and ministry workers can stand with a child who has faced temptation and responded in a Jesus-pleasing way. Make it a big deal. This is not about rewarding good choices—it's about celebrating spiritual growth.

CHOOSING TO OBEY

The choice to obey always presents the reality that there's a choice *not* to obey. God gives free will to everyone who follows Him. He does not coerce us into obedience. He loves us into obedience. Dealing with temptation becomes a key teaching ground for young believers. Bible lessons regularly present key information about temptation. However, until that information intersects a child's real life, it's easy for it to stay as head knowledge.

The choices children must make today are mind-boggling. They go far beyond what most of us experienced as children. We can't change the context of the culture our children grow up in. However, it should make us more deliberate in the way we prepare children to make godly choices and choose to obey Jesus. It's the choices they make when parents and teachers aren't looking that produce the most growth. It's the choices they make when there's no obvious "win" on the other side. Those are the character-building, heart-shaping choices. We teach our children to make good choices by building a circle of support within the family and church in every ministry opportunity.

IN THE WORLD BUT NOT OF THE WORLD

Jesus talked to His disciples about living in the world but not letting the world live in them. (See John 17:15-18.) This is a constant struggle as well as an opportunity for growth. Every child wants to fit in and have friends. However, when the desire to fit in tempts a child to choose a behavior or attitude that displeases God, it's a problem. In situations such as this, a parent or spiritual mentor can come alongside a struggling child to talk about and pray about this confusing line between being caught up in worldly pursuits and being in this world but not of it. This is also where young disciples can encourage other disciples.

Remember: God's overarching goal is a search-and-rescue mission. He needs children who are His disciples to represent Him in relationships and situations that adults cannot. You can help a child build the confidence that God trusts His disciples of every age to represent who He is. He needs their presence in places where others do not follow Jesus. He needs them to be the lantern so that He can be the light.

As parents and ministry workers, talk with children about ways to be in the world without participating in the attitudes and activities that displease God. Be honest about the difficulty of making right choices. Pray for each other. When a child can bring a prayer request about this struggle, you know you have a growing disciple.

SET FOR LIFE

Learning obedience early sets a life pattern that equips children to face what the world will throw at them. It's important to give our children the opportunity to experience the joy, confidence, surprise, strength, and help that comes through a life of obedience to God. Help children understand that obeying Him sets a positive, productive, confident, and growth-producing journey and opens all the right doors to adventure, identity, purpose, service, and a life of pleasing Jesus.

FOR PARENTS

1. How do setting boundaries and teaching obedience go to-

gether? What happens if you expect obedience without communicating boundaries?

2. How can you set an obedience goal for your family and encourage family members to achieve it? An example of this would be speaking more kind words to each other.

3. Share an example with your child about how obeying Jesus made a positive difference in your life.

4. What new ideas for teaching children to obey Jesus have surfaced for you in this chapter? How will you implement them?

FOR MINISTRY WORKERS

1. In your ministry assignment, how can you help children recognize more ways to obey Jesus?

2. How can you enlist peer support for a child who struggles to obey Jesus?

3. How can you use prayer time as a way for children to ask for and share support?

4. How can you use your life experience to share with children the positive adventure of obeying Jesus?

A DISCIPLE-MAKER'S PRAYER

Trustworthy God, help me understand that as I obey you more completely, I can parent or teach with greater effectiveness. —Following

5
MAKING PRAYER A LIFE SKILL

They devoted themselves . . . to prayer.
—ACTS 2:42

When children pray, something very honest occurs—a reality and intimacy that convicts us. They pray about what's important to them without apology. They pray for family, pets, even toys. Children, especially young children, generally don't make talking to God difficult. Theirs is a simple trust, a trust that Jesus calls us to recognize and reproduce in our own lives. However, somewhere in an aggressive craze to grow up and fit in, children can lose much of that childlike trust. In order to prevent that, or help them reclaim it, we must rediscover the reality, intimacy, and childlike trust of transforming conversations with God that we call prayer.

If the child I want to influence reproduces my prayer life, will it reproduce what Jesus wants?

We model this discipleship skill as we model other discipleship skills we teach. Praying with our children helps them learn how to pray. That brings us to the question: *If the child you want to influence reproduces your life of prayer, will it reproduce what Jesus wants?* We can't teach beyond what we understand and practice. But we can partner with a child to learn together about something bigger than we are: the transformational adventure of talking and listening to God personally.

Discipling is a mentoring-demonstration process. We can't simply tell children to pray or even tell them *how* to pray. We must pray the way we want our children to pray—honestly, intimately, and often. Let your children see that prayer is your family's first response to all kinds of issues. Without abandoning regular prayer times, add prayers of spontaneity to your life. In the same way that reading opens the human world to a child, prayer opens the spiritual world. When a child understands that God listens and values every opportunity to communicate, he or she has the potential to grow an extraordinary faith.

TALKING TO GOD

Glaphré Gilliland taught children the simplest principles about prayer in her prayer seminars. These principles easily intersect a child's life. They build the kind of foundation that preserves the characteristics of childlikeness that Jesus celebrates. They are simply—you can talk to God anytime, you can talk to God anywhere, you can talk to God about anything.

When families and ministry workers take these principles seriously, they find themselves saying multiple times throughout a day or class, "Let's talk to God about that." Impromptu prayer teaches the seamless connection between God and life. It helps children understand that God is always present and always available to listen.

Critical to teaching a child to pray are the times that are regularly set aside for prayer such as mealtime, bedtime, worship time, and class time. These are anchor times and build discipline and rhythm into a child's prayer life. These regular prayer times may involve written or memorized prayers that teach valuable models. They also give children regular times to share prayer requests. They give families an opportunity to pray for each other. Many bedtime prayers have turned into salvation prayers. Don't underestimate the value of these regular prayer times.

I have learned more about prayer from my children than I have learned over the last 30 years of my life.

—A parent

LISTENING TO GOD

Listening to God is praying too. If prayer is really a conversation with God, there has to be back-and-forth communication. Chapter 2 discussed helping children hear and recognize Jesus' invitation to become disciples. This listening doesn't stop just because a child responds by making a decision to follow Jesus. It's only the beginning of a lifelong journey to listen as a way to follow Jesus better.

In the same way that ongoing conversation is the mark of a good friendship, ongoing conversation with God sustains a decision to follow Jesus. Remind children that people who keep learning new things about each other develop a lasting relationship. Friendship rules! Whatever is important in protecting and maintaining a friendship is important in maintaining a friendship with Jesus. Teach children to talk to God about their day, their likes, and their dislikes. Then remind them to return the favor and listen.

Teaching the listening part of prayer is crucial to a disciple's lifelong journey. Prayer is not just about telling God what we want or need—it also helps us learn to listen to what God

---

Different Ways to Listen

- Don't expect all children to sit still to listen to God in silence. Some children have to be moving to focus. Take a listening walk. Encourage listening to God while doing other things.

- Some children are social and need the verbal exchange to grow their listening skills. Provide guided discussion and listening times for them.

- Children who have difficulty focusing benefit from having paper and markers. What they draw may give you insight into how they're listening.

wants. However, it's harder to teach, because it isn't a tangible voice we listen for. "Listening" is just the best word we have to describe it. Here are some principles we can use to communicate to children that we expect them to hear from God.

1. Use scripture first.

The Bible is God's story. It represents God's voice speaking to us about His story and His interaction with people. The Bible is God speaking personally. The more we help children understand this truth, the more they'll view the Bible as a person to hear and not just words to read. Explain that scripture is a good way to begin a personal conversation with God. Use scripture activities during family prayer that encourage this dialogue with God. Chapter 6 shares more ideas.

2. Share how you *hear* from God.

It's important for children to know how others understand communication from God. They especially need to know how the people they live with hear from God. Help them understand that it's an awareness that grows. Nurture their curiosity and sensitivity to this awareness.

3. Talk about *inside* listening.

Make the distinction between listening with your outside ears and listening inside. Children are very literal. Be careful about using words that can confuse them if they take the meaning literally. Explain that when God wants our attention, He speaks in a special way so that we know He's speaking. Make sure you emphasize that God will never tell a person to hurt anybody. Also, restate that anything God says will always support what He has already said in His Word.

4. Plan listening time.

Read a scripture, and follow it with a few seconds of *inside* listening. What does God want to say as we read this scripture? Give everyone a chance to listen to God to find out. Where does God want to connect it in our lives? Perhaps we've done a disservice to our children by asking what they *think* instead of asking, "What is God saying to you?"

It's God's plan that we help children hear from Him directly. After all, the shortest distance between two points is a straight line. It's that straight-line intimacy we want children to discover early and build on for the rest of their lives. While it's a parent's responsibility first, God's plan doesn't end with parents. He makes it the responsibility of others in the faith community to add their influence, teaching, and nurturing to support parents and children. The real mission is to follow God's plan—together.

TEACH CHILDREN PACT PRAYER

PACT is a simple acrostic to help children understand the components in a talking-listening time with God. In the same way we talk about a friendship *pact*, PACT reminds children that having a conversation with God is one of the best ways to grow a friendship with Him.

"P" is for "Praise."

This step of praise helps review who God is—He is our rock, salvation, helper, doctor, comforter, hiding place. He is love, mercy, justice, wisdom and so much more. It's nearly impossible to review who God is without a sense of awe and gratitude. Teaching children to start a prayer with praise is to help them remember that God is big enough, strong enough, and

---

Fun Ways to Praise

ABC: This is a good praise exercise when driving to church. Think of a word that describes God for every letter of the alphabet.

Scripture tells us who God is. Look up several scriptures, and keep them available as a way to pray and praise.

Praise songs help us thank God for being who He is. Name a favorite praise song, and sing it together.

---

smart enough to help them with whatever might be troubling or confusing them.

"A" is for "Ask."

Encourage children to ask God anything. Help them understand that God cares about everything that makes them happy or sad. We can ask for help for ourselves or for someone we care about. We don't know everything about what we ask, but we know that God does. Make sure children understand that God doesn't always give us the things or situations we want, but He always answers. That's why it's important to listen.

"C" is for "Confess."

To confess means admitting to God that you've sinned. It means that we agree with God that what we did was wrong. Confession keeps our connection with God clear. That's why it's important to make confession a regular part of prayer. We need a clear and clean connection with God so that we'll be able to understand and recognize His answers. Help children understand that it's always okay to ask God, *Did I do something that a disciple should not do?* Remind children that the only reason

God points out something is so He can forgive it and help His children follow Him better.

"T" is for "Thanks."

Thank God for the help or for answers He has already given or is going to give. There's always something to thank God for, even in the middle of hard or confusing times. Thanking God for what He *is* doing and where He *is* working reminds us that God is always present and always making a difference.

HOW CHILDREN LEARN FROM US

Children learn the importance of prayer by watching when, how, and where we pray. While prayer is a very personal conversation with God, we must not keep it to ourselves to the extent that our children don't understand the importance of prayer in our lives. If families pray only at mealtimes and bedtime, what does that teach a child about the importance of prayer? There are lots of reasons to stop and pray. If we want children to develop a relationship with God that involves an open conversation with God throughout the day, we must use that model in our prayer life and talk to them about it.

Also, remember that children respond to conversational language. Pray with children according to their vocabulary, experiences, and understanding. Just make sure you're making that heart connection with God, or they'll think prayer is about saying the right words.

Do you want children to pray about attitudes, actions, decisions, desires, and fears? Do they know that you pray about these things too? Ask them to pray for you when you face difficulties. Be specific what you need God's help with. There are many reasons to pray, but the one that catapults us into discipleship is because we want to know and do what God wants. We don't pray to *change* a circumstance—we pray for God to change *us in* a circumstance.

Always pray honestly. David learned that God desires "truth in the inner parts" (Psalm 51:6). Since God knows everything, it's impossible to hide anything from Him. The companion truth is that God will use only the truth to help. Model this as you pray with and for your children, such as *God, I really don't know what to ask.* . . . Children can tell the difference between words that are supposed to sound good and words that come straight from the heart. If it's the truth, pray it.

Keep prayer times short and focused. Accommodate a child's attention span. No one should be bored during prayer. Boredom or distraction could be a sign that the child doesn't understand the powerful connection. Put on your creative cap, and try some of the ideas in this chapter. Remember: it's not about how different you can make prayer time—it's about making the connection with God.

Be careful to not talk more than you pray. If a child presents a concern or shares a joy, stop and pray about it. Pray out loud while you drive your children to school—with your eyes open, of course. Pray during a difficult homework assignment. Instead of *promising* to pray about something, stop and pray *right then.* You'll remember to *keep* praying if you do. The pray-first strategy serves as a reminder and also teaches children that we believe that God has the most important answer in the matter.

THE POWER OF PRAYER

Nothing keeps us praying more than understanding that

something occurred that would not have happened without prayer. Families can adopt prayer projects in which each person is praying or listening to God about his or her part in an answer God wants to give. Are we convinced that praying makes enough of a difference that we dare give children a chance to think big, pray big, and perhaps stretch our faith?

Remind children that when they pray, they're talking to the Creator of the world, who understands everything about everything. This truth about God gives us confidence, trust, and unfailing belief that whatever information God has and wants to give us is exactly what we need. Who wouldn't want to connect to such unbelievable power? Raise children's sights to think about how God wants to use His power through an answer to prayer. A child who experiences the power of prayer will keep on praying.

Each evening we have special time as a family. We have a designated area in our house for this, a special-time blanket we sit on, our family Bible, and a candle we light that reminds us of Jesus' ever-present love for us.

—Angela, parent

GOD ANSWERS PRAYER

Most of our children's questions about how God will answer prayer can be answered with "I don't know—let's find out." Share your confidence that children can know what God wants to tell them. Express your belief that whatever the answer is, it comes straight from a heart of love.

While God always answers prayer, He doesn't always answer in the way we expect. Use examples from your own life to demonstrate how God sometimes says, "No," sometimes says, "Not now," and sometimes says, "Yes." When the answer is "No" or "Not yet," it usually means we'll have more questions about what to do next. Teach children to take these questions back to God. This is the way a young disciple grows in the knowledge and wisdom of God.

It's exciting when a child recognizes God's answer to a prayer. And it gives tremendous confidence to parents. It's a part of getting our children ready to face the world on their own. By helping them understand how God leads through prayer, we arm them with the best protection possible. After all, the best help for our children doesn't come from us—it "comes from the LORD, the Maker of heaven and earth" (Psalm 121:2).

We must be deliberate in helping children receive, confirm, and celebrate answers to prayer. No matter what the prayer is, God has a response. You can keep prayers in a journal and include a place to record His answers. From time to time, review and celebrate the answers. Share your own answers to prayer with children using age-appropriate language and situations. It's possible in our push to teach children to pray that we have not spent the same effort to talk about answers to their prayers.

Not only will this encourage young believers on their journeys to follow Jesus—it will also encourage *you.*

My mother had a special candle she
placed on the dining room table. When
the candle was burning, we knew someone had received an answer to prayer and
that it would be shared at dinner time. It
was an occasion for joy and celebration! It
made a huge impact on my life.

—*Sandy, ministry worker*

AGE GROUP PRAYER LESSONS

Teach prayer skills according to the way your children learn, not just the way you learned. Active children need active ways to practice prayer. Pray while you walk, jump, or bounce a ball. Children who learn by hearing should pray out loud. Children who learn visually will benefit from pictures. Social children need lots of opportunities to pray *with* others. Here are some other ideas according to age.

Infants

As you hold a baby, caress him or her, and pray aloud in a calm, loving voice. If the baby is awake, make eye contact as you pray. Even a baby will connect a gentle voice with something good and secure. Praying aloud for an infant doesn't teach him or her how to pray, but it does help parents and others who care for babies keep prayer a foundational component for all life activities.

Toddlers

Match prayers with a toddler's activity level. Take a "thank-you walk" around the house or outside. Thank Jesus for bubbles, blocks, trees, clouds, hugs, and each other. Make talking to God as conversational as talking with family and just as frequent.

Preschoolers

Begin a more formal but very simple teaching about prayer. When a concern arises, suggest, "Let's talk to God about that." When something fun makes everyone laugh, say, "Let's thank God for that." Repeat with words and actions the fact that you can talk to God anytime, anywhere, and about anything. Practice ways to stop and pray. Remember: it must be a prayer that comes from your heart too. Children recognize artificiality.

Elementary-age Children

Expect children who are learning to read and study their world to understand deep and lasting lessons about prayer. Don't underestimate the power of their prayer. Share how it makes a daily difference in your life. When Jesus convicts you about impatience or an insensitive response, confess it to the child as something God talked to you about. As this spiritual exercise deepens your prayer life, it has great potential to influence the place your children give prayer in their lives.

MAKE PRAYER CENTRAL

The best way to raise children who pray is to be a praying family. While family prayer may start with mealtimes and bedtimes, don't let it end there. There are as many ways to enjoy family prayer as there are families. The following are just a few ideas.

1. Pray scripture. Praying scripture is a wonderful way to learn about prayer. Find scriptures about God's will, God's peace, God's wisdom. Then create a personal prayer out of the words of the scripture, such as *God, help me to devote my mind and heart to the work of prayer.* (See Colossians 4:2.) This makes for good family discussion as you make a list of prayer principles. Write or type scriptures on cards for easy access. When this is a regular family habit, ask children to select a scripture to pray. Always connect a prayer principle to a real-life situation or personal request.

2. Blessing prayers. To bless someone is to ask God to make good things happen in, through, and because of him or her. Pray a blessing on your children on special days such as birthdays, Christmas, baptism, or the Sunday they join the church. Pray a blessing before they go to school or camp. Then look for ways to identify how God brought about the blessings you prayed.

3. Stop and pray. We often stop and *talk* about our children's problems or concerns. Try a stop-and-*pray* strategy. Pray first. Talk second. As previously stated, it reinforces that what you believe has more power in the life of your child.

4. Keep a prayer box or journal. Children benefit from seeing prayer's full-circle power. When you pray about something, write it down, and wait for God to answer. When God's answer surfaces, write the answer or result beside the request. Talk about the fact that God's answer is sometimes different from what we expected. When children see God's answers for themselves, they're learning the power of prayer.

5. Book bag and lunch bag prayers. Write a prayer on note paper, and slip it into a book bag or lunch bag. Then think of other ways to remind children that you're praying.

6. Prayer closets and corners. If it's true that *where* we pray is not as important as simply praying, ask children to name a different place to pray in your house or at church. Then take everybody to that place for prayer time.

Especially for Young Children

- Use a pocket photo album of family and friends to pray for people they know and love.

- Use a photo cube, and insert magazine pictures of things God made. Use simple questions to guide prayers, such as "Who made dogs? Let's thank God for dogs."

- Many plastic, cloth, and board books of prayers are available for young children. Make sure you have at least one. Consider storing it in a special place rather than just with other books.

- Echo prayers are good for young children. You say a sentence prayer, and the child echoes it. As the child becomes more comfortable, switch roles so that you echo the child's prayer.

- *The Pray and Play Bible*[1] is a unique concept that uses a Bible story as a prayer focus. Creative prayer activities for families or classes follow each story.

---

7. **Written and memorized prayers.** Take time to write a group prayer for your family or class. It could be a New Year's prayer that you pray from time to time. It could be about something you want to learn as a family or class. Prayers that are memorized offer good models and provide an easy place to start with young children. Find ways to use both written and memorized prayer to stimulate children to pray in their own words.

THE FAMILY WHO PRAYS TOGETHER

You've heard that the family who prays together stays together. There's something uniquely bonding about prayer ties. They supersede blood and marriage ties. They're that eternal connection to an eternal God who wants to make an eternal difference in each person's life. Pray together. There's no substitute. If time is your biggest obstacle, consider ways to pray when you're already together, such as mealtimes, drive times, and so on. You don't have to make it long or involved. Start that practice in some way today. Prayer connects you to every answer your family needs, because prayer connects you to God.

- Talk to children about what they pray for. Ask questions that relate to lessons about prayer, such as "What does God's Word say about this?"

- Add your sentence prayer to a child's prayer to help him or her know you're praying, too, such as *God, I feel the same way Sarah feels.* Teach other children to add a thought or agreement to a sibling's prayer by praying it.

- Pray for others. Create a prayer list for your family for the week by asking who you should pray for and how God might want you to pray for this person.

- As you read Bible stories, look for the ones that share how God delivered important messages when people prayed. Look for opportunities to connect the lesson to something in the child's life.

- Memorize the Lord's Prayer together. Talk about what it means to live it. Then take a phrase a week as a prayer focus.

- Pray the Beatitudes, and talk about how to make the characteristics of God's kingdom a description of your family.

- Pray Psalm 23 or any other psalm. Experiment with paraphrases that might relate to children better.

I asked our daughter what she learned from us about prayer. She told me that when she knew we were praying for her, she knew that God was involved. She admitted that it encouraged her to be honest with us because God knew everything, and we were talking to God.

FOR MINISTRY WORKERS

1. Ministry workers have the opportunity to give children a different social group in which they can learn about and practice prayer. Make prayer an important part of your gathering. Don't treat it as a bookend, just a way to start or finish a lesson. Make the God connection real. Pray in a conversational tone. Use the same kinds of words you use to talk to your best friend.

2. Teach a principle about prayer as you pray together. Use questions like "What happens when we pray?" One answer is that we connect with God. Ask, "If God knows everything, why do we pray?" We pray so that God can

tell us what He wants us to know or so we can receive special help or direction.

3. Use scripture to guide prayer, especially about difficult subjects. For example, the Bible tells us in 2 Thessalonians 1:12 that we should pray that the name of Jesus will spread. How can we pray about that? What might Jesus lead us to do if we keep praying that?

4. Consider some other ideas that might enrich your class prayer experiences:

   • Use prayer circles. There's something powerful about standing or sitting in a circle and leading children to pray together about something. When someone has a request, ask that child to stand in the center as a way to emphasize the support of prayer.

   • Encourage children to pray at the altar. Schedule a time in the sanctuary to talk about praying at the altar. Encourage children to pray quietly beside a friend who comes to pray at the altar.

   • Help children make praying together in corporate worship something special. Encourage them to pray for people and situations as a pastor prays, even when they don't know the person or situation. Help them think about all the power that comes from praying together.

   • Help children support each other in prayer. Teach the class to support each other by continuing to pray during the week for special requests. Use prayer reminder cards. Encourage children to follow up their prayers for someone to find out how God answered their prayers. Use prayer partners.

- Set up prayer stations. These can be different places around the classroom and can include pictures on the wall or symbols on a table with an idea about what to pray. Play quiet music, and let children choose a station and pray. You can also add activities: draw a picture about your prayer, write your name after you pray, pray with someone, write a note to a person you prayed for, and so on.

- Consider ordering *PrayKids*[2], a bimonthly, kid-friendly, undated publication designed to "encourage a lifetime of passion for Christ through prayer."

HOLY GROUND

There's a big difference between teaching the basics of a skill and teaching ways to apply that skill that result in a relationship. We can tell children when to pray and what to pray, but true prayer goes a step further. True prayer is a conversation with God. Words help us make this connection, but prayer isn't about the words we use—it's about what comes from the heart.

It's impossible to teach children about prayer without learning some lessons of your own in the process. That's the beauty of mentoring and discipling. Sometimes the student becomes the teacher. Sometimes children take the lessons and run with them. But isn't that what we want? We don't want to just reproduce *our* faith in children. We want to raise children to live with extraordinary faith in the world they're growing up in.

Prayer helps children grow in faith. It makes all the other components of discipleship fit together. When children apply their innocence, honesty, energy, and optimism to a conversation with God, stand back—you're on holy ground.

FOR PARENTS

1. Answer the question asked at the beginning of this chapter: If my child reproduces my prayer life, will it reproduce what Jesus wants?

2. How have I shared my prayer life openly with my children? In what ways do I need to do it more?

3. Which of the ideas from this chapter do I need to incorporate now?

FOR MINISTRY WORKERS

1. How have I made prayer a priority as I work with children?

2. How can I do more to encourage a connection with God when we pray?

3. How can I help children understand the value of corporate prayer in worship?

A DISCIPLE-MAKER'S PRAYER

Speaking God, help me listen more carefully to you so that the children within my influence can't wait to hear you speak. In your Son's name I pray. Amen.

6
LEARNING TO READ AND STUDY THE BIBLE

The unfolding of your words gives light.
—PSALM 119:130

The special children's speaker stood in front of a group of children and their parents. He had already won them over with his humor, simple magic tricks, and compelling stories. Now he stood in front of them with a big Bible in his hands.

"I don't know why some people think the Bible is boring," he announced. He opened his Bible while carefully turning his head to look at the far left side of the audience. When he did, flames jumped out of his Bible. Of course the children screamed and pointed with great enthusiasm. He closed the Bible and acted as if he didn't know what was going on. He continued talking about how exciting his Bible was. When he did, he turned his head to speak to the far right this time. The same thing happened again. Flames leaped out of the open Bible, and the children's excitement escalated.

Although we didn't know for sure how he did it, the parents and older children knew it was a trick of some kind. Trick or not, he made his point and went on to deepen the children's awareness that the Bible is a book of adventure, mystery, twists, and turns. As parents and ministry workers, we all wish for the flaming Bible at home so we can entice our children into its contents with more success.

Why can't children fall in love with the Bible as if compelling flames commanded their immediate interest? How can we encourage their curiosity to find the truths that make positive differences in their lives? How can we help them understand that the Bible is more than a group of printed words or historical compilation or even a textbook of information to learn? The Bible is a living interchange with a living person.

Christian parents understand the importance of the Bible and want it to be central in their family life. Sunday School teachers use it as their source for every lesson. Children's worship leaders use scripture and stories from it. The pastor preaches from it every week. Everywhere children go in church, the Bible is front and center.

Shouldn't that make it easy for children to fall in love with it? Not necessarily. Too many times there is disconnect between the stories and lessons of the Bible and using it to guide actions and attitudes.

So what makes the difference? What encourages children to embrace the Bible as the most important reading they'll ever do in their lives? There's no single answer to that question, but there are some understandings that encourage the love relationship to take place.

The Bible tells us who God is. We study Abraham's story and find out that God is a promise-keeper. We study Jonah and discover the intensity of God's passion for those who don't know Him or have turned away from Him. Every story tells us something new or reinforces something we already know about God. When we come to the New Testament, we come to the most important picture of God we have—Jesus! As one child put it, "Jesus is the best picture God ever took." God—His love, His mission, and His holiness—is the subject of every story and letter. Keep Him the main character as you read and study the Bible with children. The Bible makes God bigger than life, because He is. We should do the same.

The Bible is the living Word of God. The Bible is not just a book of good words or wise words. It shares God's Word. God gives the same powerful, creative word that made the heavens and earth to communicate with us. Nothing boring about that! Hebrews 4:12 reminds us that "the word of God is living and active." How do we help children know this? The best way is by what God's active Word does in our lives. What living, active work is going on right now in your life because of God's Word? Teaching children what God's Word *says* without sharing what

God's Word *does* degenerates into head knowledge. God doesn't share himself through His Word so that we know more; He shares himself through His Word so that we'll let His Word change us.

The Bible is a book of truth. We want our children to know the truth and be set free from anything that's not true. (See John 8:32.) Helping them discover God's Word as truth that fits any age, period, or culture is critical to their discipleship and spiritual independence. When children fall in love with God's truth as the guiding beacon for their lives, they grow in ways we couldn't make happen even with the best parenting or teaching skills.

AN IMPORTANT LESSON

A Bible study leader challenged a room full of mothers to help their children develop a love for reading the Bible with the same determination for encouraging them to read in general. She was right. I was completely dedicated to help my daughter Lisa read. Did I think she would naturally transition her reading skills to the Bible on her own? That's when I found controlled vocabulary Bible story books to match different reading levels. It was just what I didn't know I needed. Lisa was reading similar books in school. When I gave her the first Bible story reader, she was excited to read Bible stories for herself. As her skills improved, I continued to find Bible story books to match her reading ability until she could read the Bible.

Unlike other issues in discipleship, Bible reading and Bible study depend on some basic academic skills. Until a child has an ability to read, even the *New International Children's Bible* is just something to carry. Since the Bible needs to become important to children from the very beginning, we can't wait for reading ability to be an accomplished skill before we introduce the Bible to children. Here are some ways to bridge the gap.

- Start with simple Bible story books and collections designed for beginning readers. Some of these books work for children who are learning to read or function as a first reader. They may also state the reading grade level. (See Appendix for examples.)

- Let the child use the Bible story book the way older children use the Bible to read and study a Bible story.

- Use a read-together approach. You read a sentence, and then your child reads a sentence. The *Read Together Bible*[1] color-codes this process for you.

- Start with Bible story books that retell the Bible story without adding extra information or details.

- Make sure that the main character in the Bible story is God. The Bible tells us what God is doing.

- Keep asking your Christian publishing supplier for information about new resources.

FOR YOUNG CHILDREN

It's important to find ways to introduce the Bible to young children before they can read. Collect Bible story board and cloth books like *My Bible Book*.[2] Check out Bible story collections, especially ones designed for toddlers and preschoolers. They have limited text and colorful pictures. Read the stories, or simply talk through the book, allowing the child to point and ask questions about the pictures. Use craft items from church to guide a young child to retell the story. Keep some of these in a special place to use whenever you read the story again from a Bible story book. Developing a love for God's Word through His stories is a great place to begin with young children.

STARTING TO READ THE BIBLE

It's exciting when children begin to read. They no longer have to put their world together for themselves. They can see it through other eyes. That's especially true of learning to read the Bible. The Bible helps us see life through God's eyes. People can tell us what the Bible says, but something very personal happens when we read it for ourselves. It becomes a personal conversation with God. We no longer get the information sec-

---

Bible Skills

Grades 1-2

Teach the child the difference between the Old and New Testaments.

Teach the child to locate a few books on his or her own: Genesis, Psalms, the Gospels, and so on.

Teach the child to memorize simple verses.

Grades 3-4

Teach the child to find a verse in the Bible by its reference and read it.

Teach the child to begin guided Bible study.

Grades 5-6

Teach the child to use a concordance and other Bible research tools.

Teach the child to begin independent Bible reading and study.

---

ond and third hand. We get it right from the one who was there when the story happened.

That's what makes reading the Bible different from reading any other book: the author shows up—every time. God interprets and illuminates His Word so that it becomes a personal message. Helping children understand how to receive this personal message as they develop their reading skills is a critical part of discipleship.

Reading is a skill that takes several years to develop as a useful tool for reading the Bible. The Bible is not the easiest book for new readers or someone who has trouble reading. I applied a grade-level reading test to Luke 2:1-4 from the *New International Version* and found that it's written at an eighth-grade reading level. That means that some children will struggle to read the Bible for themselves because of their reading abilities. As parents and teachers, we must make loving God and His Word the priority. Reading is one way to do it, but consider other ways.

- Use audio versions of the Bible on tape or CD. (See Appendix for examples.) Let a child *read along* after hearing it.

- Practice reading a simple Bible verse with children before you ask them to read it aloud.

- Memorize a verse, and then help your child read it from the Bible.

- Investigate children's translations of the Bible. (See "Bible Versions for Children" sidebar.)

- Use a Bible designed for English as a second language.

- Make every out-loud and silent reading experience as positive and successful as possible.

In Sunday School classes, be sensitive to different reading levels. Offer the translation that is easiest for most children. Keep one or more Bible story books for beginning readers. Pair a reader with a nonreader. Allow children to volunteer before asking anyone to read aloud. This is another place where the partnership between home and church helps. Often ministry workers can offer more resources at church to help children explore Bible versions and Bible study resources. However, without home support to connect the Bible to experiences in real life, the explorations may feel more like school lessons than an adventure that encourages a love for God's Word.

WHAT ABOUT BIBLE VERSIONS?

Today we have many translations and paraphrases. Make sure you know the difference. A translation goes to the original language and makes the closest word-for-word translation possible. A paraphrase starts with a translation and uses contemporary language and contexts to update it. Paraphrases tend to use longer, more involved sentences that make them more difficult for some children to read. However, they may also use simpler vocabulary. The best plan is to select a basic translation. Children need the repetition of hearing things over and over, the same way each time, as they build their understanding and love for the Bible.

MY BIBLE

Make having one's *own* Bible something special for children. Ask them to bring their Bibles to family time. Encourage them to take their Bibles to church. Read from *their* Bible. Give them simple research projects. Offer Bible activity book-

Bible Versions for Children

- The *New International Version* (NIV) was completed in 1978 by 115 Evangelical scholars. It has become the best-selling English version and is a very reliable translation.

- The *International Children's Bible* (ICB) was completed in 1985 by 21 Evangelical scholars and is written on a third-grade reading level.

- The *New International Reader's Version* (NIRV) was published by the International Bible Society. It is another children's version, also on a third-grade reading level.

- The *Contemporary English Version* (CEV) is a 1995 translation by the American Bible Society especially for children. It's also a good ESL (English as a Second Language) version.

lets that require that they use their own Bibles to answer questions. Make digging into the Bible fun as they develop their reading and study skills. Be careful not to overdose on the creative activity aspect without emphasizing God's presence in His Word. Without the connection to God, the Bible becomes just another book to study.

THE BIBLE'S IMPORTANCE TO FAMILY LIFE

The Bible becomes an important part of a child's life by making it an important part of family life. Read from it; pray from it; use it to answer questions. Keep a family Bible with important dates for family births, baptisms, graduations, and so on. Share something from the Bible to celebrate birthdays and other special days. The more you use the Bible *together* to engage the family and meet real needs, the more children understand that the Bible is the best Word for life. Here are some other ideas:

- As you read from a Bible story book, show children where the story is found in the Bible.
- Let children find in their Bibles the scripture you plan to read.
- Let children hear often, "What does the Bible say about that?" and take time to help them discover the answer.
- Read through the Bible by stories.
- Have a Bible verse for the week or month.
- Memorize scripture together.
- Review the Scripture lesson from Sunday School or worship service during the week.
- Play Bible games.
- Find ways to reinforce Bible lessons from Sunday School, children's worship, quizzing, and so on.
- Select a life verse for each child. Use it to talk about spiritual growth in their lives.
- Help children find the scripture in their Bible during worship.

Get excited when children initiate a Bible-to-life connection. That means they're experiencing spiritual growth. To understand what the Bible says is one thing, but to connect what the Bible says to a real situation in life is the mark of true discipleship. Discipleship is always more about lifetime than class time.

TEACHING CHILDREN TO STUDY THE BIBLE

Most children won't dive into the Bible to find an answer to a life question. It usually takes one-on-one time to develop their interest in independent Bible study. The challenge for families who want to do it together is accommodating different skill levels. However, trying to find the time to work with each child individually can become a scheduling nightmare. The best practice is somewhere in between, alternating individual and group coaching. Remember: the idea is not skill mastery as

---

Bible Study Resources

A **children's Bible encyclopedia** is an A-Z listing of people, places, and vocabulary with definition, description, or explanation.

A **Bible story book** is a chronological collection of key stories from the Bible.

A **children's Bible dictionary** is a short definition of vocabulary as well as identification of people and places.

A **life application/study Bible for children** introduces books of the Bible with background, with information about people, places, and practices. It usually includes questions to spur application.

A **concordance** lists almost every person, place, or key word from the Bible and gives references for where it can be found in the Bible.

A **topical index** lists topics from the Bible and shares references for where to find what the Bible says about that topic.

Online resources provide many reputable Web sites that offer translations, pictures, concordances, a topical index, commentaries—everything needed for Bible study at no cost.

---

it is in school. The goal is helping your child achieve a love relationship with God. Keep the first thing first as you equip your child to find out what the Bible says and means.

Even if Bible study is new to you, you can still help children learn about the Bible. Learn as you go with children. What could be more exciting than that?

Teach simple skills first. Teach the difference between the Old and New Testament with games. Teach how to find a book in the Bible using the table of contents. Help them understand how to find a verse by its "address"—the chapter and verse.

Make study resources available. Purchase a one-volume children's Bible encyclopedia. Computer-savvy kids will enjoy online study resources. Study and application Bibles contain many helpful resources. Teach children how to look up Bible words using a concordance.

BIBLE STUDY METHODS

There are many ways to study a Bible passage. Any plan that engages children for personal application is a good one. Bible study investigates a passage or book to find what might be missed just by reading. Find a simple study plan that captures the most important information so that a child can use it immediately in a life situation. The following are two possibilities.

The 5W Plan

The 5W Plan is the journalistic approach. It applies the who, what, when, where, and why method—the method news writers use to gather information for a story.

WHO is in the story? The obvious answer is "anyone named in the story." Sometimes minor characters in the story also have background and relationships that give us insight into what's happening. Get children thinking about people who aren't mentioned. Might children have been present but not mentioned? When a child thinks about the story from the perspective of someone his or her own age, it keeps it personal.

WHAT is happening? Was a meal involved? Did someone ask a question? Did an argument develop? Is this a teaching story? Look for action words. Sometimes more than one thing is happening.

WHERE did it happen? While Bible research requires that we understand important details about where a story occurred, we need to keep children focus on application. They can answer the *where* question by simply identifying the city, the house, or the hillside.

WHEN did it happen? When was the letter written? When was Quirinius governor of Syria? Don't concentrate only on historical timeline. Was it first thing in the morning? Was it early in the week? Was it in the middle of a special celebration? Was it a happy day? A sad day? A hot day? A normal day?

WHY is it in the Bible? Why did Jesus respond the way He did? Why did God ask someone to do a certain thing? Why were people confused? Why were they happy? No matter what other *why* questions children answer, make sure they end with *Why do I need to understand this?*

Be careful that you don't overwhelm beginning Bible students. The personal application is more important than the process. Each "W" question could become a study in itself; don't let it. Keep things simple, and help children make discoveries for themselves.

This 5W Plan is a good one to use in group study. Divide a

large group into small groups, and assign each group a "W" question. Make sure everyone in the family or class has an opportunity to make personal discoveries and take personal responsibility for an application step.

The SOAPY Method

The acronym SOAPY helps children learn a Bible study method that's easy to remember. It's one way to think of the Bible as soap in your life—to clean you.

"**S**" is for Scripture. Write down the Scripture passage. Use a short Bible story, especially as children begin learning the method.

"**O**" is for observation. What stands out in this story and why? Is it the compassion of Jesus? Is it the crowd's reaction? Make a list of these observations.

"**A**" is for application. What does God want me to do because of what I observed? Should I speak out about someone's kindness? Should I share something of mine with someone else?

"**P**" is for prayer. How can I pray these lessons so they become part of my life? Write a sentence prayer about what I need to apply.

"**Y**" is for yes. Can I say yes to what God wants me to do? This step of personally affirming the Word of God is very important. It teaches children about taking responsibility for *doing* something about a lesson or instruction.

ENCOURAGE INDEPENDENT LEARNING

There are few other skills in learning to follow Jesus that are more important than learning to study the Bible for oneself.

That's true for children and adults. Independent Bible study is the goal for us and for our children. We start by giving them the skills, practice, and coaching they need. Then we encourage them to use these skills to find their own answers in the Bible. While all of us need help to unlock difficult truth, maturing as a follower of Jesus means that the follower is growing as an independent learner. It's the "aha" moments that allow a person to become this kind of learner. It takes more than jotting down the right answer or completing fill-in-the blank review sheets.

Do you remember when something in God's Word made its first clear intersection with your heart? Do you remember how powerful that understanding was? Didn't it make you want to find something more? That is what propels children into independent discovery. We provide the possibility for this discovery with ideas, skills, and simple structure. However, only the Holy Spirit and a child's receptivity to His communication will provide the arrow that makes the bull's-eye.

USE QUIZZING

Quizzing[3] is an exciting way to study God's Word. Children study six books of the Bible in one particular first-through-sixth-grade program. They participate in fun, non-threatening competition that gives points for correct answers. It incorporates two skill levels. The Red Level is for beginning readers and children who need a simpler approach. The Blue Level is for children with better-developed reading, study, and processing skills. The beauty of the Bible quizzing ministry is that it isn't actually necessary to participate in organized events to profit from the material. The material offers an invaluable resource for Bible study at home or in any small-group setting. Make sure you model the level of engaged learning you want for the children. If you aren't learning anything new, the children won't be challenged to do so either. Share how a hunger for God's Word makes you excited to dig deeper to find out what you missed last time you read this story. Help children understand that the Bible is a bottomless supply of understanding and help. No one is ever too old to study the Bible.

No matter what method or material you use to help children learn to read and study the Bible, make allowances for different styles. Don't assume that the way you learned to study the Bible is the best way. Give active learners something to do to answer the questions, not just something to write. Draw a picture. Make a timeline on the wall. Tape a map on the floor. Play a game. Let visual learners study pictures and draw them. Let tactile (touch) learners handle puppets and cut-out characters. God is a master at understanding individual differences. Let Him help you individualize your approach.

HIDING GOD'S WORD

Because we don't carry our Bibles with us everywhere we go, it's important to memorize key scriptures and passages. Technology has made so much information available at our fingertips that we've become negligent in emphasizing memory work. Now more than ever it's important to memorize God's Word.

Memorizing God's Word helps plant it in the hearts and minds of children where it can continue to grow and the Holy Spirit can use it to shape their lives. Memorize Psalm 23, the Lord's Prayer, the Beatitudes, the Ten Commandments, as well as specific other scriptures.

NOT JUST ABOUT STUDY

Falling in love with God's Word is not just about spending more time in study. Children will get the wrong idea about God's Word if we make them think they have to study a lot more. Many children are already overwhelmed at school. Instead, we can give them the chance to see immediate results in their lives as they apply something they've learned. Parents have an advantage over ministry workers in doing this, because parents can match a story or passage to real-life needs. They can affirm any attempt to put into practice a Bible lesson. They can help connect Bible to life until the child begins to make the connections on his or her own.

Here are some other ways to engage children in learning from the Bible separate from set-aside study time.

- Read a scripture in the morning, and talk about ways God can use it in life during the day.

- Read the Bible aloud. It was written to be read aloud. Let different members in the family read "parts" by assigning Bible-character dialog to them. Talk about what can be learned about God's love, direction, warning, compassion, and so on.

- Read stories from the Bible about the families of Moses, Jacob, David, and others. These stories teach many things about being a loving family.

- Create a favorite Bible verse collection for the family.

- Keep a notebook of how your family has received help and instruction from the Bible.

- Read one Bible story per week so you can talk about different aspects of the story every day.

- Memorize scripture together, and find ways to share memorized scripture with each other during the week.

- Find a topic list of quick references to read when you're feeling sad, confused, lonely, or happy, or make one that fits the needs of your children.

- As you share parts of the Bible with your children, ask yourself, *What will the children do with this information on their own this week?*

- Use *Connect.*[4] This is a family devotional guide complete with Bible study activities for children, questions for discussion—all you need in one booklet.

A REAL PARTNERSHIP

Every area of discipleship profits from teamwork between home and church. Ministry workers cannot be totally responsible for discipling children who are growing up in Christian families. They'll have their hands full standing in the gap for children who come from families who don't follow Jesus.

Ideally a balanced partnership will exist between home and church. When Sunday School classes teach basic Bible study skills and parents reinforce those skills at home through daily life experiences, something very special happens: children begin to recognize a connection between their lives and God's Word.

It's important to set the bar high—not for children but for ourselves. We can't reproduce in our children what they don't see happening in us. Do we demonstrate our passion for God's Word? Do they see us searching for God's answer to a life issue? Do we make them hungry to read God's Word and hear what He has to say to each of us personally? As we live our lessons from God's Word—fresh from time in His Word—children recognize our authenticity. It's through that authenticity that children fall in love with the Word of God. It's not about our skill or our knowledge or our creative activities; it's about allowing children to see that God's Word helps us love and parent better.

The same is true for ministry workers. Think "active," "alive," "sharp," "penetrating." Is that the way you know God's Word? If it is, you'll pass on your love for God's Word to the children you teach and work with.

FOR PARENTS

1. What living, active work is going on in your life because of God's Word? Have you shared it with your children?

2. What ideas will help you encourage your children to learn to read the Bible for themselves?

3. What resources could you add to your family library to help children read and study the Bible for themselves?

4. How can your family learn to study and memorize the Bible together?

FOR MINISTRY WORKERS

1. How do you communicate your love for God's Word as you work with children in your ministry assignment?

2. Do you have a graded approach to teaching Bible reading and study skills? If not, how could you develop one?

3. How can you initiate a healthy partnership between parents and the church as it involves Bible reading and study?

4. How do you adapt for different learning styles as you try to increase Bible study skills?

A DISCIPLE-MAKER'S PRAYER

Living Word, speak your Word to me so that I won't be in danger of sharing empty words with the children whose lives I influence. In Jesus' name I pray. Amen.

7
DISCOVERING THE JOY OF GIVING GOD ALL

Each one should use whatever gift he has received to serve others.
—1 PETER 4:10

Fifteen adults showed up for work day at church—fifteen adults and one four-year-old. It wasn't a last-minute change of plans because babysitting didn't work out. This was intentional. Four-year-old Caleb came with his dad to work. What can a four-year-old do? He can shovel bark into a wheelbarrow for others to spread. With his child-sized shovel, he worked tirelessly. Encouragement from Dad and others helped, but Caleb had his own sense of mission. This was his church, and he was helping to take care of it.

No child is too young to learn the joy of helping God take care of His world and His Church. It's the starting place for developing ministry leaders. It shapes an others-centered perspective. You don't have to use the word "stewardship" to be involved in teaching the responsibility, joy, and privilege of joining God's plan for taking care of everything He created. Stewardship is the foundation from which a disciple discovers and uses every ability, interest, and spiritual gift.

STEWARDSHIP IS . . .

The simplest way to define stewardship for children is this: it's how we take care of everything God has given us. It's about caring for the world, our family, every possession, even our jobs. We own nothing that didn't belong to God first. Every possession and opportunity comes from something He made and makes available to us. He shares resources and abilities and life itself with us as a part of His plan to take care of every person and thing.

Stewardship is an important way to protect children from feelings of entitlement and self-centeredness. It teaches that we own nothing. God loans His resources to us. Since everything belongs to God to begin with, He has the first word about how we use His resources.

Stewardship is about understanding God as a generous God. We understand that becoming a follower of Jesus is automatic enlistment in the army that God employs to take care of His world. Children like to belong to something big. It's an easy trait to use in teaching them how to participate in God's family as someone He trusts to take care of His world. God eagerly recruits their help.

It's easy for children to grow up thinking that everything they have comes from their parents and other family members. That's why parents are the best ones to correct this misconception. They must demonstrate their belief that everything they have and enjoy comes from God first. It's their model of stewardship that children reproduce. That's scary, because most of us want children to reproduce the biblical model. When parents live the biblical model, they increase the possibility that their children will live it as well.

Practicing stewardship isn't only about what we do for God; stewardship brings growth-producing characteristics into the life of a disciple. The byproducts of stewardship are responsibility, gratitude, teamwork, and generosity. What parent doesn't want their children to grow up with these characteristics? However, teaching the individual components is not the same as teaching stewardship. Teaching the *characteristics* of stewardship is *person*-centered, while teaching stewardship *itself* is *God*-centered. To insure a God-centered approach to stewardship, use the following key principles:

1. Everything I have belonged to God first.

This is the foundational message of stewardship. We teach this lesson as we practice a litany of thanks with babies and young children. We teach this with every surprise gift and opportunity that comes into our families. We acknowledge that God is the ultimate source of every good and perfect gift. (See James 1:17.)

2. God is generous with His resources.

Acknowledging God's generosity and personalizing it is the first step to reproducing His generosity. We must guard against taking God's generosity for granted. He gives what

He has, and He gives it freely. When children understand this, they want to give back to God. That makes stewardship a joy rather than a duty.

3. God asks us to take care of everything He has made.

Children love big jobs. Connect taking care of pets to God's plan for caring for animals. Connect recycling to caring for God's world. Help children understand that every chore, every service project, every school lesson prepares them to take care of God's world and the people in it.

4. God asks that we give to Him first.

"First" is an important concept to children—first in line, first piece of dessert, first turn. Being first is important in a child's world. Teaching children that God deserves the first part of everything reminds them that God gave first. Giving Him the first thoughts of the day, the first tenth of money, the first use of any special ability keeps God in first place.

ALL, NOT PART

In some ways, teaching stewardship makes every part of discipleship easier. A disciple fully belongs to God. There is no thought, no activity, no time of the day, no friendship that doesn't come under the Lordship of Christ. That's what being a steward means—being under higher orders.

It's important to help children understand that God wants all of us, because He gives all of himself to us. We get the bigger gift, because there's always more of God than there is of us. That's the adventure we can help our children see. Besides, the more we give to God, the more He trusts us with. We become conduits to transfer more of God's resources into the world. He gives to us so that we can give to others.

Sometimes we teach stewardship backwards. We teach what children are supposed to do—give something away whether it's money, time, energy, or a possession. But the real message of stewardship is not what *we* give—it's what we've already received. God gives each of us exactly what we need to serve Him. The companion truth is that God always gives us enough to share. No one is ever too poor to share something.

TEACHING TITHING

My dad taught me about tithing before I could do the math. My sister and I stuffed envelopes for our pastor-father and received a dollar for completing the job. When Dad paid us, he gave us a tithing envelope and helped us with the math. He always paid us in coins so that we could remove one-tenth to put in our tithe envelope. On Sunday when the offering plate came to me, I proudly placed my envelope in. It wasn't about the amount—it was about making my own contribution. Thanks to God's generosity, I had ninety cents to add to birthday money and allowance I was saving.

There's no better way to teach the faithfulness of God than with tithing. When young disciples understand that money is just another resource God gives, they can join the excitement of seeing how far God's money goes. Biblical tithing is giving to God one-tenth of what you earn. It's an act of simple obedience.

Usually the first money children earn is an allowance. It's essential to connect allowance to tithing. It keeps tithing as the priority lesson in money management. Start an allowance to give children an opportunity to give to God from their own money. Then look for ways to keep tithing central to your family's giving:

RAISING KIDS TO EXTRAORDINARY FAITH

- Give allowance in a way that children can separate their tithe easily.
- Make sure each child has tithing envelopes. If your church doesn't provide them, consider ordering some or preparing your own.[1]
- Encourage children to prepare their tithe as soon as they earn money from allowance or small jobs.
- Make sure children see you place your tithe into the offering.
- Talk about how and when you started tithing.
- Share how God blessed your obedience.
- Talk about tithing as God's plan to take care of His Church.
- Use Bible stories that teach God's plan for giving.
- Purchase the "So . . . You Want to Give to God?"[2] pamphlet, and download the free leader's guide.[3]

While parents have the primary responsibility to teach tithing, ministry workers can play a part in increasing a child's desire to practice giving God's way. Emphasize God's principles in Bible stories about giving. Practice the math of tithing with the use of play money. Keep tithing envelopes available in your classroom, and help children prepare their tithe. Give children opportunities to share with each other how God surprises them with His generosity.

Be sensitive to the possibility that God may want to teach children the value of generosity early. Never get in the way of a child's desire to practice God-prompted generosity. God blesses their obedience. He trusts obedient disciples with more resources. Help children look for the ways God gives back His blessings. Make sure that children understand that we give because God gives, not because it's a rule. It's His example we follow.

Tithing is the minimum we give to God. It pleases God when we give other offerings. Encourage children to make contributions to missionary offerings, building fund pledges, and other special offerings. Participation is the key. Help children understand that we can always give more together. Ministry workers can help children understand how their giving makes a difference by translating amounts into tangible things. How many nails for the building project will a certain amount purchase? How many meals for a missionary will a certain amount buy? Or better yet, target a specific item and raise the amount together.

LASTING RESULTS

Most adults will tell you that when they practiced tithing as a child, they continued the practice as adults. Besides, it's just plain good money management. God will never direct anyone to spend more money than He gives. One who gets excited about giving to God rarely falls victim to our culture's debt-producing consumer mentality.

NOT JUST MONEY

Stewardship isn't just about giving money to God. Since children aren't big money-makers, this is good news. Use family and class time to talk about the many different ways you can share what you have with God and His people. It could be the gift of time, smiles, encouraging words, help, abilities, energy—whatever the child knows how to do. God isn't a talent scout looking for the best and brightest. He looks for the faithful. All you have to do is share what you can. He never requires what you don't have.

A family who enjoys finding ways to give to others is usually more giving and forgiving with each other. Generosity develops a heart for compassion. Every family is a stronger family when they take time to do something for other people. In chapter 8 I'll share more specific ideas about serving others.

SHARING SPECIAL ABILITIES

Every child has a special ability. It might be a personality trait such as endurance, sensitivity, patience, flexibility, cheerfulness, or any number of others. It can be special skills in art, music, athletics, or academic areas. God is very efficient. He never gives a special ability or trait to anyone to be wasted or hidden. On the other hand, He doesn't give them to make anyone any more special than He already created them to be. Make sure that children understand that it's not about doing something better than anybody else. Everyone has something important to contribute. Helping children find a place to contribute within the family and the community of faith is critical. Here are some helps for leading children to see their abilities through God's eyes:

- God is the source of all abilities. (See Deuteronomy 8:18.)
- God gives each person a special ability. (See 1 Peter 4:10.)
- A special skill or ability doesn't make you more important than anyone else. (See Romans 12:3.)
- God has a purpose for each ability. (See 1 Peter 4:10.)
- No one should use abilities in ways that separate people. (See Ephesians 4:3.)

- The primary use for any ability is to serve God and others. (See Acts 11:29.)

- Since abilities come from God, we must follow His instructions about how to use them. (See Romans 14:12.)

- Because abilities are tools, it's our responsibility to keep the tool developed, sharpened, and ready. (See Luke 12:38.)

It's easy to understand how to use musical ability for God. But what about athletic ability or math ability? Children need help from Christian adults to enlarge their vision about how

---

Ways to Discover and Encourage Skill Development

- Have "praise days," and encourage children to use abilities to praise God.

- Organize athletic or art camps.

- Create broad categories and noncompetitive processes in talent discovery festivals.

- Interview Christians who have different skills.

- Pair a child with an adult who has a skill that interests a child.

- For every children's event, list ways children can use their abilities to help.

- Be sure to affirm personality traits as often as you affirm abilities.

- Explore behind-the-scenes opportunities such as stuffing worship folders, preparing Communion elements, and so on.

every ability is useful to God. Use athletic children to support the importance of teamwork in projects. Use them to help younger children learn athletic skills. Use a math whiz to collect money or keep attendance statistics. Find out what children do well, and help them learn how to serve others using their abilities.

Since children are still growing and developing, their abilities may not always be obvious. I didn't identify my ability to write until I was in college. Some abilities take more time, experience, and schooling to surface. This is why families and ministry workers need to provide lots of opportunities to explore different skills. Childhood is for exploring many different abilities to find interest and skill connections.

ESPECIALLY FOR MINISTRY WORKERS

Ministry leaders who plan opportunities for children can keep the following things in mind:

1. **Teach worship-*leading*, not performance.**

Even for those who have special drama, music, and instrumental skills, teach them something they won't learn anywhere else. Teach them that sharing the ability is a lot more fun when you use it to help others love and praise God.

2. **Teach doing your best, not being the best.**

Our culture puts a lot of emphasis on being the best. The freeing message for children is that God doesn't choose us based on any best thing about us—He chooses us because He loves us. Sometimes success doesn't mean winning the trophy. Sometimes success means showing up and following through and making the contribution you can. Think what would happen if children chose activities based on what God wanted them to learn from it. Maybe children would tackle the world with more confidence if they were encouraged to do it God's way.

3. **Don't encourage competition.**

That may mean rotating opportunities in "lead" roles. It might mean calling it something other than audition. It might mean doling out affirmation for everyone. It might mean making committed involvement, not perfection, the goal.

4. **Model servanthood.**

Servants usually don't choose their assignments. Model positive attitudes when your service assignment isn't about using the things you do the best. Serving is about helping where there's a need.

SPIRITUAL GIFTS

I stood before a group of fourth through sixth-graders to present a lesson I had presented many times. It was about gifts—God's gifts.

God wants to give you a special gift. It's something that only God can give you. He won't give it to anyone else in the same way He gives it to you. There's a catch: you have to be a member of His family. And you have to follow the instructions that come with the gift. What do you think? Do you want a gift?

Their responses were predictable. Everyone wanted a gift. I continued explaining.

This gift won't come in a package to unwrap. It's something God gives on the inside. It's a gift that will help you do something special for God in the way that only you can do it. The gift doesn't make you better than anybody else, and it doesn't make anybody else better than you. God picked it out just for you. That's what makes it a special gift.

Then I share my favorite verse about spiritual gifts. "God has given each of you some special abilities; be sure to use them to help each other, passing on to others God's many kinds of special blessings" (1 Peter 4:10, TLB). Spiritual gifts are gifts God gives someone when he or she becomes a member of His family. He gives them so that each person has a God-designed place within the family of God. They help God's people fulfill His command to present ourselves as living sacrifices as a way to thank and worship God. (See Romans 12:1.) They're *His* gifts. He designed them. He tells us how to use them. They complement personality and any natural or genetic propensity toward activities and involvements.

Children are not exempt from receiving spiritual gifts just because they're young or immature. However, since they're still developing in every way, it may be easier to identify natural abilities before spiritual gifts. This is why building on an understanding of stewardship is so important. When children are already using everything they have for God, they're probably already using a spiritual gift—even if they don't know what it is. Helping children learn to do everything for the glory of God is the critical discipleship lesson here. (See 1 Corinthians 10:31.)

SPECIAL GIFT VERSUS NATURAL ABILITY

It's easy for children to think about spiritual gifts from their experiences with natural abilities. Natural abilities are things a person does well. These include activities like singing, athletics, art, and playing instruments. These come from God, too, because He created us. It's not that one is more spiritual than the other. A spiritual gift helps a person use his or her natural abilities in ways that please God. It's not as important to distinguish the overlap between natural ability and spiritual gift for children. It's more important to teach them what God's purpose is—to serve His family.

Some children's natural abilities surface more quickly than others, and this can create feelings of competition or feeling left out. Helping children understand that God gives *everyone* a spiritual gift is an encouraging truth that can help them with these feelings. When someone becomes a follower of Jesus, God makes a spiritual investment in that person. He gives that person the desire, the sensitivity, and the energy to join Him in accomplishing His mission on earth. The beauty of God's plan is that it works perfectly with any natural ability a child already has.

The idea is to *discover* spiritual gifts. Childhood is a wonderful time to try out different roles and responsibilities within the community of faith to find the right ministry involvement. While it is not a good idea to pigeonhole a child by telling the child what spiritual gift he or she has, it's helpful to provide information about spiritual gifts and offer a variety of opportunities for exploring spiritual gifts.

THE GIFTS

It's fun to disciple young believers in this area. This isn't about head knowledge. It's about serving others and finding a good fit. This kind of exploration is fun and non-threatening to children, and it's full of the variety that children like.

There's no one list of spiritual gifts. First Corinthians 12:7-11, 27-31 lists nine, and Romans 12:3-8 lists seven, depending on the translation and definitions. Five show up in Ephesians 4:11. Here's a way to identify spiritual gifts and to help children understand them:

Wisdom (see 1 Corinthians 12:8): using information and ideas to share God's will.

Knowledge (see 1 Corinthians 12:8): understanding, retaining, categorizing, or analyzing information in ways that please God.

Faith (see 1 Corinthians 12:9): trusting God and helping others to trust Him.

Healing (see 1 Corinthians 12:9, 28): accomplishing what God says will make a difference to someone who's sick, hurt, or in physical or emotional pain.

Miracles (see 1 Corinthians 12:10): performing signs and wonders through God's power to help people believe that God is who He says He is.

Preaching (see 1 Corinthians 12:10, 28; Romans 12:6; Ephesians 4:11): sharing God's Word boldly.

Discernment (see 1 Corinthians 12:10): understanding information and choices from God's perspective.

Communication or Language (see 1 Corinthians 12:10): speaking or writing about God in ways people easily understand in their own language.

Teaching (see 1 Corinthians 12:28; Romans 12:7; Ephesians 4:11): helping others understand how to study and apply God's Word.

Helping (see 1 Corinthians 12:28; Romans 12:7): serving others so that they better understand God's love.

Administration (see 1 Corinthians 12:28): organizing people to help them accomplish something for God.

Mercy (see Romans 12:8): acting with compassion and encouragement when someone is in need.

Generosity (see Romans 12:8): cheerfully and eagerly sharing what you have with others.

Leadership (see Romans 12:8): knowing what needs to be done to accomplish a project and inspiring and instructing others to get the job done.

Evangelism (see Ephesians 4:11): knowing when and how to share God's salvation plan so that others might become part of God's family.

ON PURPOSE

God's purpose for spiritual gifts is always about serving others in His church. There's no other reason God gives them. As you expose children to God's gifts, always connect them to God's purpose. The following is a good list to start with:

- **Spiritual gifts keep us humble.** (See Romans 12:3.) There's no place for competition, pride, or jealousy with God's spiritual gifts. They're not about us and what we can do—they're about what God enables us to do.

- **Spiritual gifts are to help God's family, the Church.** (See 1 Corinthians 12:7.) When everybody uses his or her spiritual gifts according to God's purpose, everything that God wants accomplished gets done.

- **Spiritual gifts accomplish unity.** (See Ephesians 4:11-13.) This is about having the same purpose, not having the same ideas.

- **Spiritual gifts make us servants.** (See Ephesians 4:11-

12.) Every spiritual gift helps us share something with someone else.

- **Spiritual gifts bring about spiritual maturity and Christ-likeness.** (See Ephesians 4:13.) The more we use spiritual gifts according to God's purpose, the more we think as Christ thinks, act as Christ acts, and love as Christ loves.

DISCOVERING AND SHARING SPIRITUAL GIFTS.

Remember: the goal is discovery. Make the discovery process an exciting adventure. Rather than studying the different gifts, encourage children to practice them within their family and church. Children can be interested in a lot of things that they're not especially good at. It's more important that children understand their places in the family of God than being able to name their spiritual gifts. This helps parents and ministry workers do more than just get children involved or get them up front. It helps connect them with the *purpose* for God's spiritual gifts. It requires that we ask important questions each time we give children a ministry opportunity:

- Did you encourage or help someone?
- Did you help someone understand God's love better?
- Did you bring people together?
- Did you experience God's love?

A PLACE TO SERVE

Give children as many opportunities to serve as possible. Pair them with an adult in ministry. Don't just ask children to do a job—give them a spiritual mission. Prepare the adult who works with the child to use conversation and affirmation to help the child know what it means to do something for Jesus. It's not important to make sure that each child serves according to a spiritual gift. Let children learn the value of using their interests, natural abilities, and acquired skills to serve God and His people.

- **Let families serve together.** After the ministry opportunity, take time to talk about what each person does best, enjoys best.

- **Introduce children to serving opportunities outside the church.** They can serve in nursing homes and children's hospitals as well as helping with community clean-up projects or any other community service project.

- **Organize adult and child partnerships.** Children can be greeters, runners, servers, pre-session Sunday School volunteers, or nursery helpers.

- **Give children simple organization projects.** Ask them to organize a contact process by telephone or e-mail.

After children have taken part in different activities and ministry involvements, ask: what did you learn about yourself? What did you learn about the activity? How do you think God wants to use this involvement to help others? Would you do this again? Why or why not?

I have seen children begin to develop
their spiritual gifts by drawing pictures
for the bulletin, singing in church, making cards for the shut-ins.

—*Stephanie, children's pastor*

Teach spiritual gifts as a journey, not a destination. The goal is not to figure out for children what their spiritual gifts are. The goal is to help children learn everything that helps them find their places in God's world. When that's the focus of your discipleship training, no one but God is in charge of the lessons.

THE GRATITUDE ATTITUDE

Connect every act of kindness, help, encouragement, and hard work to the grateful activity of a steward. Children need opportunities to experience that it really is more blessed to give than to receive. You're developing their sensitive eyes and compassionate hearts. Make sharing their time and energy something fun. Always divide responsibilities at a children's event so that children take part in "giving back" service. Supply child-sized implements for young children to work alongside adults at a church work day. Play music while you work together. Sing silly songs. Make working together something fun, and you'll learn why God loves a cheerful giver!

Thank You, God!

- Help children write thank-you notes to people who serve the church, especially in children's ministry.
- Find a "Give Back" project in the church that your family or class can be responsible for.
- Purchase and read the book *77 Ways Your Family Can Make a Difference.*[4]
- Help children make every performance-oriented activity about giving what you have to God.

Directing children to give back to God is at the core of life-long following. We can never outgive God. His love and generosity shares with us everything we need to do His will. Who really needs more than that? Giving back becomes a privilege and a joy. Duty will never develop what God wants to grow in His disciples. Only love will. Helping children discover God's generosity and encouraging them to look for ways to share His resources with others are priceless ways to shape the next generation.

Fast-forward through the years to see what your family or class might look like in 10 or 15 years. Are the children you influence learning enough about stewardship today that they'll live it in the future? Will they have collected enough lessons about the extravagance of God's perfect gifts to keep looking for ways God meets their needs? Will they be givers or takers? Will they be hoarders or exporters? Think of employees working at their jobs with a steward's mentality. Think of the new lay leaders who will share their God-given resources to join God's mission in their world. Teach them the gift of using everything they are and have and do for God. Raise them to give more than we did. The world they will live in will need it.

FOR PARENTS

1. Take an interest survey in your family by asking each member to fill in the blanks:

   Something I do well is _____

   _____.

   Something I would like to learn is _____

   _____.

   Use responses to provide opportunities for children to practice their abilities and explore new ones.

2. What will my children learn about stewardship by watching my life?

3. Which of the ideas to keep tithing central do I already practice? Which could I incorporate?

4. How have I or will I encourage my children to use their abilities for God first?

FOR MINISTRY WORKERS

1. How can I offer opportunities for children to explore new ways to use their interests or abilities through drama, music, art, writing, cooking, sports, and so on?

2. How can I divide responsibilities to give more children a chance to serve?

3. How do I reduce the spirit of competition in my ministry area?

4. In what areas do ministry workers and staff directors need to make a plan to provide more opportunities for children to serve?

A DISCIPLE-MAKER'S PRAYER

Faithful God, help me raise kids to extraordinary faith by using your resources. —A determined follower!

8
HELPING CHILDREN TAKE THEIR PLACES IN THE FAITH COMMUNITY

Work at telling others the Good News, and fully carry out the ministry God has given you.
—2 TIMOTHY 4:5

It's important that young disciples understand that being a disciple is never a solo experience. The very essence of the story of salvation brings people together, gives each new believer a ready-made family, and offers an amazing interconnectedness of generations, history, and experience. No other decision in life does this in a way as powerful and far-reaching. Whatever we do as we help a child follow Jesus, we must raise his or her sights to see the big picture, the cloud of witnesses, the cheering section. It is for both encouragement and accountability.

So what does it mean to be a member of the family of God? What does it mean to the parent who wants spiritual growth to parallel physical, mental, and emotional development? What does it mean to all of us who provide the safety net for a young believer with questions and inconsistent obedience? We have the opportunity and privilege to connect children to a global circle of support that's available to them anywhere in the world. When a child makes the decision to follow Jesus, he or she joins the family of God around the world as well as the historical family of God. That's a big deal!

Church is a community of believers,

not a spiritual drive-through.

—Diane, preschool director

This aspect of discipleship training requires first-person participation. It's important for young disciples to experience what it means to be accepted in the family, do family things together, and experience family support during difficult times.

For our children to experience this, the church family must be very intentional in introducing this concept. As parents and ministry workers, we must make sure that we participate relationally with our church family. We look for ways to give our children a broad exposure to the local and global family of God. We can't raise disciples by ourselves. God never expected us to.

EXPOSE CHILDREN TO CHRISTIAN ROLE MODELS

Children need to hear how the missionary heard a call to take God's message to other parts of the world. Find Christians who have succeeded in the skills and careers that interest young believers. Read aloud the biographies of Christians who made following Jesus their passion and made a difference in the world because of it. A child will find heroes and role models somewhere. We want their role models to be Christian.

Practicing Accountability

1. Identify a spiritual goal such as memorizing a scripture to live it or adopting a more loving attitude.

2. Make age-appropriate adaptations so that each child can participate.

3. Talk about ideas that will help each person be successful.

4. Plan a regular time to report back.

5. Affirm all progress toward the goal.

6. Affirm honesty about difficulties.

7. Talk about how a plan to report back makes it easier to focus on the goal.

PRACTICE ACCOUNTABILITY

Spiritual accountability demands that we report our progress, success, or difficulty in keeping the promise to follow and obey Jesus. For this to work in powerful ways, all of us who work with children must be accountable for our attitudes and actions—parents to children, children to parents. Discipleship and spiritual growth thrive where there is accountability.

Accountability happens best in small groups. Look for ways to establish positive and supportive accountability within your family. When you share a devotional thought that has a life application, tell children when you'll ask them what they've done about it. Older children may be ready for a more organized approach to accountability, so consider meeting with them weekly for 10 to 15 minutes, the time involved to run a short errand. Identify key accountability questions such as the following:

- What did you read in God's Word this week?

- What did you do about it?

- What are you praying for this week?

Ministry workers can make the same kind of commitment in the work they do with children. Consider ways to raise accountability expectations. If you close one session with a challenge about living a scriptural lesson, start the next session by asking for a report. Since the group will include children who have not yet started their discipleship journey, be careful not to expect more from these children than they're ready for. Emphasize the importance of support and encouragement. Take turns dividing into groups of two or three to ask accountability questions and pray for each other. Make sure it's a non-threatening experience. This is an opportunity for growth and a way to add excitement and passion about living God's truth. Practicing accountability is one way to protect against the disconnectedness that can occur as we present lessons from Sunday to Sunday. There must be a life connection to translate into spiritual growth. Accountability makes life connection a priority.

Mark 6:30 reminds us that accountability was an important part of the disciples' life: "The apostles gathered around Jesus and reported to him all they had done and taught." As we gather for accountability, it should be done with eagerness instead of dread.

MENTORING

While mentoring is not a discipleship requirement, it can be a structured way to encourage and shape the spiritual growth of a young disciple. It can also be an important way to address discipleship for children who don't have Christian nurture at home. It is a one-on-one process that requires voluntary acceptance and accountability on both sides. It starts with a relationship of honesty, acceptance, and a love for finding out how Jesus wants us to live. It can involve simple Bible study, or it can occur around planned but informal conversation about relationships, problems, or fears. The mentor must be ready to share scripture and scriptural principles rather than simply give advice. It will often require digging into the Bible together to find out what it has to say about a certain issue. Mentoring may address a short-term crisis, or it can turn into a relationship that spans childhood to young adult life. Ministry workers are probably the best people to identify the needs and interest for mentoring.

MAKE INTERGENERATIONAL CONNECTIONS

Every family has members of multiple ages with aunts and uncles and grandparents and great-grandparents. These connections shape a child's understanding of the larger world, a world that has a past as well as a future. The same is true in the family of God. Some churches organize "Prayer Partners," "Friends in Christ," or "Special Friends," for example, as a means of establishing partnerships between children and adults. These are rich opportunities, some of which fill a larger role in the lives of children than anyone ever imagined. These intergenerational pairings don't come directly out of the activities and classes designed for children. These are connections that ministry staff

---

"Special Friends"

- Ask for volunteers who will get to know and pray for a specific child for a year.

- Create a profile for each child that includes birthday, special interests, his or her photo, and so on.

- Schedule a get-acquainted time before, during, or after a regular church service.

- Encourage the adult special friend to send messages of prayer support regularly.

- Suggest that the adults find a time to share their salvation stories and ways God has made a difference in their lives.

- Change "special friends" annually unless there's a special request.

---

intentionally form to make sure children have the opportunity to know people they might not otherwise meet. Children require more support than what their parents can give to live as a disciple. This is one way to make sure they have it.

WHEN THE FAMILY GATHERS

The family of God gathers to worship each Sunday. Children should be led to understand that worship is not about attendance, filling a seat, or keeping very still. We give our hearts and minds to God during the time that's set aside for worship as we think about God in ways that turn into gratitude and praise. True worship is its own magnet. Why would children want to go anywhere with us where they are required to just sit still and be quiet? On the other hand, why would they not want to participate in a powerful expression of loving God? Why would they not want to experience the presence of God as He keeps His promise to meet with every attentive and receptive heart?

Make gathering for worship the highlight of your week. Begin this teaching early. As parents, make sure that the activities you allow in a service help children focus on God, His goodness, and His gifts. For very young children, it could mean a Bible story book or Bible coloring book. Early elementary children can draw pictures of what they hear and see. Encourage all children to participate in singing. Help them find the place in the Bible so they can read along. Some churches offer a special children's worship folder. Hold hands as a family during prayer time. Help children worship according to their understanding and attention span. The worship experience doesn't stop at church. Talk about it on the way home and at the next meal. Talk about key lessons or scripture during the week.

RAISING KIDS TO EXTRAORDINARY FAITH

If your children attend a special children's service, talk about what parts of the service helped them worship God best. Get permission from the ministry leader to accompany your child to children's worship. Then take your child with you to the adult service. Talk about different ways to worship.

THE SUNDAY SEARCH

Radio minister and father of four David Mains initiated a family activity that became more than a routine in the lives of his children: the "Sunday search." It involved three questions: (1) How will Jesus speak to me? (2) How will Jesus speak through me? (3) Who will I tell? He talked to the family about searching through every part of a worship experience to find how Jesus spoke to them. On the way home from church or during lunch, the family had a chance to share their answers. The parents began to realize that when the children knew they were going to be answering these questions, they began to be more intentional about using worship to listen to Jesus. It also required the parents to be more intentional about participating fully through worship.

MAKING SUNDAY SPECIAL

While church attendance is certainly something God commanded, He doesn't want anyone to do it out of duty or tradition. Instead, treat every Sunday as a mini family reunion. How do you prepare for that weekly family time? How do you talk about it? How do you get ready for it on Sunday morning? Karen Burton Mains reminds us in her book *Making Sunday Special,* "If Sunday is not a day that is so special that we and our children look forward to it with delight, then we are neglectful parents."[1]

Making Sunday special is a parent's responsibility and should not be left to the pastor or worship leader or Sunday School teacher. God deserves our enthusiasm, our focus, and our praise, so we should set the behavior and attention standard high.

Here are some ideas to make Sunday special in your family:

- Light a Sunday candle during lunch, and talk about the Sunday search.

- Have a special family devotional activity.

- Do something special as a family: take a walk, visit someone in need, share time with another Christian family.

- Protect Saturday nights, and prevent late nights and irregular bedtimes.

- Make a Sunday bag for young children with items to help them worship God in their own way.

- Start building excitement for Sunday on Saturday. Plant expectation.

- Listen to Christian music while getting ready to leave for church.

- Play a Bible quiz game on the way to church, or sing fun Bible songs together.

- Streamline Sunday mornings by taking care of clothes and meal plans on Saturday.

MORE THAN SHOWING UP

Discipleship training should include involving children in ministry to others. Otherwise, children may grow up in church with the idea that everyone else is supposed to do something for them. It is impossible to be a disciple without taking responsibility within the family you've joined. Jesus kept teaching His disciples to recognize needs, reach out to people, and do the work necessary in the kingdom of God. We can do no less for our children.

Let children hear from people who use their spiritual gifts to serve others. Find adult ministry volunteers who will allow children to shadow them for a Sunday. Talk about the results in class or with the family. As ministry workers, interview different ministry leaders as a regular part of gatherings. Better yet, let children interview them.

Prepare children for a ministry assignment. Meet with them for short training. Make it important. Talk to them about what they can learn through their ministry assignment.

If they help greet, give them instructions about making people feel happy to come to church. Affirm them by telling them how they encourage people in ways that we cannot.

There are endless ways children can have regular ministry assignments. Most of them may resemble apprentice relationships, in which you pair a child with an adult. For example, let a child help an usher, learning about seating people and passing offering plates. Give early arrivers special jobs to straighten Bibles and hymnals in the pew backs, sharpen pew pencils, and so on. Give them a responsibility at a church dinner. Don't overlook more creative tasks. Some children are artistic enough to help with poster-making and bulletin boards. Others are techies and thrive on computer projects. Make sure they understand the ministry component and not just how to complete the task.

Parents can also help in this area. Where are you already involved in ministry? Where can your children help you? When I took my turn in preschool, I always invited our daughter, Lisa, to join me. I made sure to spend time telling her about the lesson and activities. I gave her special jobs. Then afterward we always talked about what happened. She gave me feedback that helped as I planned another time.

Every child needs a ministry responsibility in the church. Here's a list to get you started:

- Find a family project. This can be a short-term or long-term involvement, and it can piggyback on something you're already doing. Try something new together. Use it as a way to model how disciples can use different spiritual gifts and abilities within the same ministry role.

- Give everyone a responsibility. This is appropriate for families and classes. Who clears the table? Who is in charge of handing out the books? Adopt the philosophy that every child has a job. Teach how big jobs get smaller when everyone helps.

- Develop children's ministry teams. How about a welcome team made of several ages? How about a children's council? How about a camp or VBS publicity team? How about using sixth-graders to be news gatherers and reporters for a children's newsletter?

- Organize a ministry fair for children. Write down as many jobs as you can think of on index cards, one per card. Use pictures or props for non-readers. Allow children to sign up for one ministry job for a month or two at a time. Consider using sixth-graders as captains for some jobs.

- Plan "serve days." Involve the whole church or at least the families from the children's department. Organize several service projects for the church and local community. These could involve anything from clean-up projects to visiting shut-ins to working at the church. Have a family captain for each project. Sign up ahead of time. Return to the church for pizza or hot dogs.

KEEP THEM LEARNING

Talk with children regularly about their ministry involvements. As much as possible, make serving others fun, but be sure they stay focused on why they serve rather than how much fun it is. Ask questions such as *What did you learn about yourself? What did you like best about what you did? What was easiest? What was hardest?* Affirm their willingness, their perseverance, their on-task focus. Identify anything special you see beginning to surface, such as a leaning toward mercy, discernment, or administration. Keep encouraging them to ask God to show them how and where He wants them to serve.

A PLACE FOR CHILDREN

When children are engaged in specific ways within the life and ministry of the church, they share their childlikeness with us. Jesus made it very clear that children could teach us a lot about the kingdom of God. They teach us innocence, simple trust, unpretentious honesty, along with enthusiasm, energy, and optimism. God placed them in our midst to help us understand how He values childlikeness.

We make a place for children when we affirm what they share with us when we work together. Many times their faith eclipses ours. Their pure enjoyment of simple things helps us pay attention to the beauty and intricacies of this world that we often take for granted. Their ability to give wholehearted focus to the thing at hand reprimands our ineffective multi-focus. Where do we need their perspective and how can we give children an opportunity to share it? This is where ministry workers play the biggest role. They must constantly be looking for ways to share a child's perspective to remind the family of God what childlikeness is. The following are some ways you can make this happen. Keep adding to the list.

- Interview children about their understanding of God, how God answered a prayer, or what happened when they obeyed God's Word.

- Give people an opportunity to intersect with children through intergenerational events and learning activities.

- Let children teach adults something they've learned—a song, a verse, or the hand motions that go with either.

- Collect answers from children about faith, church, God's will, and so on. Share them in written form.

SUPPORT CHILDREN'S INTERESTS

Nothing defines a loving family quite like celebrations. Make sure you have a good way to celebrate children's achievements. A celebration is an important way to help children feel valued in a family.

Celebrate special awards and achievements. Celebrate Christ-honoring attitudes and actions. Chronicle their achievements in church communications.

Attend events that are important to them. This is essential for those who work with children. Imagine a child introducing you to his or her coach or teacher by saying, "This is my Sunday School teacher," or "I want you to meet my children's pastor." That person understands that you value that child. What bridge could begin from that simple understanding?

ADOPT FAITH PROJECTS.

Jesus said some things happen only by exercising faith. What are we missing by not asking God for some faith projects? Kids are activists. They want to be a part of something bigger than they are. God has plenty of projects that will keep our children challenged. He needs followers who are willing to take on faith projects with kids. Only He can identify and instruct about those projects. Faith projects help children find the answer to the question "What can we do for God that only God can help us do?" Connecting children to an adventure for God

---

Finding a Faith Project

- Ask for ideas about choosing a faith project.
- Instruct children to spend time asking God which faith project He wants them to participate in.
- Remind children to ask God before doing anything toward the project.
- Talk about faith lessons often.
- Celebrate every accomplishment as God's empowerment.

---

is just the thing to engage their imagination and enthusiasm and set them on a lifelong pursuit of service.

Family faith projects can involve anything that affects the family. For instance, an upcoming move could become a family faith project. Challenge children to pray for the right house and neighborhood. Or make tithing or a special offering a family faith project. Ask God who you should reach out to in your neighborhood. Don't make it just about doing nice things for someone else. This is about learning how to following God's instructions and timing to see what happens. It's music to any parent or ministry worker when children start saying, "I think God wants me to . . ." This is the sound of a disciple in the making.

Take on faith projects as a class. Raise money to sponsor a child in a world area through Nazarene Child Sponsorship.[2] Just make sure that everyone understands that the goal is not raising money—it's to learn about faith. It's about finding and accessing opportunities that only God gives.

HELP CHILDREN BECOME DISCIPLE-MAKERS

Coming to faith in Christ has two important purposes. The first is to receive the gift of salvation and live the eternal connection to God. The second is to share it. Some people have expressed this purpose by asking what the value of Christianity is if it isn't worth reproducing. From the beginning of time, God has been spreading His message of love and redemption. This is not an option like an accessory you decide to add to your car. This is the unmistakable plan of God. You become a disciple to *make* a disciple. There must be a balance between living discipleship and making another disciple, or else it becomes a very self-centered, inward focus.

Children are natural evangelists. They'll invite anyone to their house or church. We have to be careful not to manipulate this social side of their innocence. But we also need to be careful that we don't squelch it with our own reticence. We can help them by giving children reasons to invite their friends. We can go out of our way to make their friends feel accepted and comfortable. But disciple-making goes farther than inviting a friend to church. We can help children have spiritual conversations with their friends. We can help them talk about the faith that directs their lives.

Mary heard the gospel shared in my class, responded to the invitation, and prayed to receive Jesus as her Savior. Because Mary knew I always shared the gospel each week, she brought her sister the next week, and Mary's sister prayed to receive Christ. A few weeks later, Mary brought a friend, and that friend wanted to accept Jesus as her Savior too. Mary asked if she could sit with us as I counseled her friend. After we were done, Mary said to her friend, "Isn't that the best thing that ever happened to you?"

—*Gloria, Good News Club teacher*

> If a parent tells a child to tell their friends
> about Jesus but the child never hears a
> parent tell his or her friends, it teaches a
> lot more than the message heard.
>
> —*A parent*

The easiest place to begin having these conversations is within your family and children's ministry involvement. Give regular opportunities for children to share—

- How and when they became a disciple.
- How following Jesus changes their focus, attitude, and actions.
- What God is doing in their lives right now.

We need to talk with children about ways they can share their spiritual lessons with others in the family of God. The more they routinely talk about their lives as disciples of Jesus, the easier it will be for them to have these same conversations with friends who are not disciples.

When a child makes a new decision to follow Jesus, involve another young disciple in meeting with and praying for the new believer. Some older children can even handle working through the "So . . . You Want to Follow Jesus?"[3] Bible studies with very little supervision, especially if they worked through them as new believers. What an opportunity for young disciples!

As a family or class, keep a list of first names or initials of children's friends and relatives they pray for. Join them in praying for the right opportunity to share their faith at the right time. Ask for updates regularly.

If you train children not only on how to understand the gospel for themselves but also on how to teach it to someone else, you multiply your efforts.

—Reagan, children's pastor

Suggest that children tell their friends how they handle difficult situations by praying to God for direction and help. Sometimes this offers an opening for more conversations. Make home and church a place where children feel free to express their spiritual concerns for others in their world.

Help children learn to share the gospel. Use the ABC plan from "My Best Friend, Jesus."[4] Purchase "So . . . You Want to Share Jesus?"[5] and download the Leaders Guide. Consider working with ministry staff to present the children's musical *Splash Kingdom.*[6] Everyone learns to make a gospel presentation in this musical. Investigate evangelism tools such as the EvangeCube[7] or Kids' EE-Cube[8] as visual aids as you work with children to share their faith with others. Find an approach that works for your age group. Memorize it together. Give children opportunities to role-play sharing their faith. Send children into their world to be disciple-makers.

In our 4th- and 5th-grade classes we taught the kids how to tell a friend their "story "in 30 seconds. They talked about what they were like before they met Jesus, why they decided to follow Jesus, and how they're different now that they have Jesus in their lives.

—Jill, children's pastor

INCREASE CHILDREN'S GLOBAL VIEW

The electronic communication revolution puts the whole world at the fingertips of children. Television parades the world before their eyes with every news broadcast. However, that doesn't mean that every child has a global view of his or her place in the world. Children need help to learn what it means to be a disciple in the global community. They need help personalizing the vast amount of information available.

Every time a missionary makes a presentation in your church, make sure he or she has primary contact with children. Ask missionaries to talk about the lives of children in the part of the world where they serve. Sign up for missionary e-mail letters that give up-to-date information about different parts of the world. Take your family with you to meet the missionary personally.

When a natural disaster occurs, pray for children and their families. While it's not necessary to be overly specific about the tragedies, it's important to help children do something about the disasters they see and hear about. Collect supplies for "crisis care kits."[9] Pair a children's class with an adult class who will match the funds or supplies they collect.

Involve children in some form of hands-on mission experience. Take them to local mission endeavors. Adopt a family project to sort clothes at an inner-city clothes closet. Take them with you when you deliver food to a food bank. Consider participating in a mission work project as a family. Volunteer at a small church's Vacation Bible School.

When children study different world areas, go online to explore the mission work there. Pray for the missionaries there. Put up a world map. When a news item features a country, write the name of the missionary on a flag, and place it on that country. Do whatever you can to help children understand that God's mission is world-sized. That's why He wants to mobilize every disciple to join Him in making more disciples.

Understand that as children explore different ways to find their places in the community of faith, they'll have to step beyond what's familiar and secure. Pray that these experiences will be positive ones. Pray that they'll never be afraid to step out of their comfort zones to do something God directs. Pray that they value new experiences even when they feel they do poorly or it feels awkward to them. Communicate that there's always something for a disciple to learn. God doesn't waste anything. This is discipleship training at its best.

THE WORLD WAITS

The world is desperate for positive leaders and role models. You have the opportunity to participate in supplying the biggest need for the next generation. You're influencing new disciples to take their places in the worldwide community of faith. How they hear God, how they perceive their responsibilities, and how they collect valuable experiences in ministry will shape who they become. There's no better time than now to raise ordinary kids to extraordinary faith. The world waits. We have to be about our Father's business.

FOR PARENTS

1. How can I incorporate spiritual accountability into my family?

2. Who were my spiritual mentors? How can I encourage my children to learn from other Christians?

3. How could I incorporate the "Sunday search" to help my children experience authentic worship?

4. What local or world ministry can we participate in as a faith project?

FOR MINISTRY WORKERS

1. How can I encourage intergenerational connections with the children I influence?

2. How can I give children more opportunities to serve?

3. How can I accomplish a balance between helping children become disciples and encouraging them to be disciple-makers?

A DISCIPLE-MAKER'S PRAYER

Master Disciple-maker, if you loved the world so much that you sent your Son to die for us, I should be able to answer your call to make disciples, starting with my family and any other children I influence. —A disciple-maker in training.

9
NEVER
STOP
DISCIPLING

Follow my example, as I follow the example of Christ.
—1 CORINTHIANS 11:1

How did Jesus take 12 ordinary individuals and turn them into men of extraordinary faith? How did He make the difference in three years? What's the transformational secret? If only it were a set of lesson plans that we could follow to guarantee that the children we parent and teach would become lifelong disciples. If only we could send them to a special school that did it for us.

On the contrary, the answer to raising children to extraordinary faith is the same as Jesus used. Be intentional. Be present. Open your life with absolute honesty. Depend completely on God for every word, direction, and idea. Consider every opportunity as a sacred one. Make obedience to God the natural rhythm of your life. Make prayer the transparent expression of an intimate relationship with God. Expose everyone you influence to the transforming relationship you have in Christ.

That's why discipling another person is different than simply parenting or teaching. It's more about sharing your life than telling someone else what to know or do. You must be the disciple you want another to be in order to make a disciple. Anything less is hypocrisy.

When kids own their faith and know why they're in church, discipleship becomes much easier, because they want to live life God's way—not just because their parents want them to, but because *they* want to!

—Jill, children's pastor

Several metaphors can be used for the discipling relationship between adults and children. It's coaching work. It's mentoring. However, the metaphor that gives us the most encouragement is the one that comes from a very familiar parable.

SEED-PLANTERS AND GARDENERS

Jesus told the people about the farmer who went out to sow seeds. We know the story. Some seeds ended up in unreceptive places such as rock and the sun-baked dirt turned hard and in-hospitable. Some seeds proved to be quick-growing, only to succumb to heat and drought. Then there was the field, freshly prepared to receive the seed. I think that's where most of the seed landed—in a place where seeds were expected, where they had everything they would need to grow.

Jesus calls us to be seed-planters in the lives of the children we parent and teach. Part of our work is preparing their hearts to receive God's seed. We must commit to early watering and fertilizing to maximize the growth potential. While we aren't responsible for what a child does about the seeds we plant, we're responsible to keep planting seeds.

> I planted the seed . . .
>
> but God made it grow.
>
> *—1 Corinthians 3:6*

We've explored what those seeds are. Here's our planting guide:

- Nurture a desire and expectation to hear Jesus' invitation to follow Him.

- Equip a new believer with an understanding of the spiritual disciplines that will grow a believer into a lifelong follower of Jesus.

- Teach that a decision to follow Jesus is a decision to obey Him.
- Engage children in the practice and joy of ongoing conversations with God that we call prayer.
- Present the Bible as the living Word of God, and connect children to God himself, not just the stories or lessons.
- Help children understand that God gives them abilities and spiritual gifts so that each of them has a unique place to share in the family of God.
- Encourage each child to find his or her place in the local and global community of faith.
- Empower children to become disciple-makers.

This is not just about raising good children, children with positive behavior, children with exemplary characteristics. This is about raising children who live, act, think, and love as Jesus does. They fall in love with Him so deeply that they begin to get their information about how to live as disciples directly from Him. That's the goal: independent learning, independent following, independent growing.

In order for this to be a seamless process between parents, teachers, and children, we should set high standards for ourselves. We have to live with the spiritual consistency, transparency, and integrity that we want our children to grow up with. That is a non-negotiable requirement. The good news is that God promises growth when His seed falls into receptive soil. The miracle is that it grows far beyond what we planted—30 to 100 times more. (See Matthew 13:23.) That's a big return on our investment! Is there anything else we can do in the lives of our children that can reproduce that extravagantly?

It takes many spirit-filled adults
to disciple a child.

—*Jeri, ministry worker*

THE OBSTACLES

There are obstacles, of course, to this mission of disciple-making. We live in an over-scheduled world. Parents become tired as they juggle family and work responsibilities. Broken marriages divide children's time between two parents. Growing numbers of single parents are overwhelmed with home, family, and work responsibilities. Then there are the sideline parents, who make God and church a positive "addition" to their very secular lives.

God promises to bless our obedience. He has given us all the time we need to do His will. Sometimes we must figure out what activities are draining our time and energy from what is most important. God will communicate where we need to carve out time, reduce activities, and refocus strategy.

Some obstacles will not go away easily. As the divorce rate rises and economic pressures challenge, it places more and more of our children at risk to figure things out for themselves. That means that all of us must be ready to fill the gap and support struggling parents and children. Adopt a single-parent family, and let them join you as you build discipleship strategies within your family. Invite children who live without Christian nurture to participate in key discipleship activities of your family, especially at Christmas or Easter.

Ministry workers can come alongside a child in a difficult home situation to fan into flame any beginning spark of wanting to live a life of following Jesus. While no one can ever take the place of a parent, God often uses surrogates to come beside someone in need of spiritual guidance. Whether it's by an organized mentoring plan or an informal commitment, we need to make sure that every child has access to someone who takes discipling him or her seriously.

ONE ON ONE

One of the reasons that discipling children isn't easy is that it requires one-on-one time. Without individual coaching, we can't expect a child to simply "catch" the right idea about Bible study or how the scriptural lesson and life come together. Only by spending dedicated, intentional, and prayed-for time with a child can we be part of the process God wants to use. We must pray that God will order our time so that busy lives and crazy schedules aren't our undoing. Someone teaching about physical exercise said, "You can always do something, and something is better than nothing." Take the same advice, and apply it to discipling the children you influence.

I believe children have a hunger to go deeper with God. We often underestimate their commitment and desire to being faithful, growing disciples.

—Janet, children's pastor

THE DISCIPLE-MAKER'S TEST

Use the following to evaluate your commitment to discipling the children within your circle of influence. When you know your score, choose one or two of the statements and turn them into goals for the next month. Then periodically go through the list again to increase your commitment to discipling children.

Read the following statements, and respond with one of the following evaluations: 5-always, 4-most of the time, 3-some of the time, 2-not enough, 1-never.

		5	4	3	2	1
1.	I understand what my role in discipling children is.					
2.	I'm willing to ask for help from another parent or ministry worker when I feel overwhelmed about my spiritual responsibility to raise or teach a young disciple.					
3.	I have opportunities and make opportunities to have a spiritual conversation—not a teaching session—with a child.					
4.	When a child talks to me about a difficulty in life, I stop and pray with him or her.					
5.	I open the Bible with a child to look for answers to a family, friendship, or other problem he or she asks for advice about.					
6.	I use the sacraments of baptism and Communion to help children affirm their faith in Christ.					
7.	I have basic resources for age-appropriate Bible reading and Bible study for my children.					
8.	I've shared my salvation story with my children.					

9. I know what my spiritual gift is as a starting place for recognizing a spiritual gift in a child.					
10. I know how to share the salvation message with a child.					
11. I'm praying for the opportunity to share the salvation message with a child.					
12. Our class/family celebration of Easter and Christmas reflects more of God's story than society's secularization.					
13. I have a spiritual accountability plan that I use with the children I teach/parent.					
14. I pray with my children about their spiritual growth during the time we're together as a family/class.					
15. I help children find a way to serve others.					
16. I talk about giving to God in our family/class.					
17. I encourage children to share their faith with others.					
18. I practice intentional worship and help children find their way to worship God as well.					
19. The spiritual growth of the children I raise/ teach is more important to me than their happiness.					
20. I connect Bible stories and scriptural lessons to real life, theirs and mine.					

85-100: You're making discipleship a key priority. Keep it up!

70-84: Discipleship is important to you. Find ways to increase its priority.

55-69: Discipleship is something you want to do better. Let God and others help you.

Below 55: Consider this a wake-up call. Begin now to make discipleship the priority God wants it to be.

CREATE A PLAN

Discipleship won't happen by accident. It must be an intentional activity—and that requires a plan. It can be very simple, but it should be written down so that you can refer to it often. Start by answering the simple questions below.

- How can I set aside time to pray about how God wants me to disciple the children I parent or teach?
- What is one step I can take soon that will make discipling an obvious priority in my family or class?
- What resources do I need to help me?
- At the end of a day or a class session, what question will best evaluate how discipleship has been a priority?
- Who will I be accountable to for this plan?

Living as disciples is a shared journey. We learn together.

Remember: make any conversation about discipleship a conversation about "us," not "you." Talking to children about what "you should do" defeats the primary component of discipling. Living as disciples is a shared journey. We learn together. Everybody is a learner, and nobody is the expert. Adults, teenagers, and children share personal discoveries with each other that lead to spiritual growth.

A word of caution for parents: There are a lot of parenting issues where we do not give children a choice. However, discipleship is not one of them. We use God's model. He gives His children the choice to follow Him. We may set spiritual boundaries about behavior, but we must remember that becoming a follower of Jesus is a matter of the heart and will. Living and growing as a disciple is a choice. Make sure that you don't force children into discipleship activities when they've not made the decision to follow Jesus. If you do, you may have compliance without spiritual transformation.

If we don't teach children to live a Christ-filled life, they might experience the moment of asking Christ into their lives but have no idea how to follow through with it.

—Dawn, ministry worker

THE GREAT COMMISSION FACTOR

Parents must understand that Christian parenting is Great Commission parenting. By God's standards, we have no higher reason to be parents than to make disciples. Great Commission parenting requires a personal commitment to live the surrendered, obedient, growing life of a disciple of Jesus. You can't pass on to children what's not already a part of your own life. Great Commission parenting begins in *your* heart, where Jesus sets the agenda for everything.

For ministry workers, this means that we become Great Commission teachers and children's workers. We actively look for ways to build bridges to introduce a child to a personal relationship with Jesus. We teach more than Bible stories and fun activities. We connect children with an extravagant God whose love and resources have no end.

We make sure to communicate that a relationship *with* Jesus is completely different from knowledge *about* Him.

You can't pass on to children what's not already a part of your own life.

THE PARTNERSHIP

The empowering truth is that discipleship is something we do together. God's plan works with great effectiveness. Parents introduce children to God, His plan, and His ways. Ministry workers deliver the same message through different activities and guided learning. The extended family of God shares its affirmation and support and opportunities for service. When children hear and see the same message everywhere—that discipleship is the *life* of following Jesus—the Holy Spirit uses that repetition to awaken the seeds we planted. The roots begin their anchoring journey. Growth starts showing up in ways we can see, affirm, and celebrate. Right before our eyes a young disciple grows! What a privilege to be a firsthand witness and front-row cheerleader!

The whole church family should be in the business of discipling our children.

—Belinda, children's pastor

TO CHANGE THE FUTURE

What might happen if we recommit to the call of Jesus to make disciples, beginning with the children? What might happen if we engage our energies and creativity to help children hear and respond to the invitation of Jesus early? What might happen if children really believed that following Jesus was the most exciting way to live to the fullest? They would enter adolescence with spiritual armor. Their spiritual growth would parallel every other area of growth in their lives. They would be better equipped for the enlarging independence of their adolescent and young adult lives.

We have an unequalled opportunity to help children make lifelong decisions to follow Jesus. We can become partners with the Creator, who takes the innocence of a child and grows a spiritual conscience that shapes him or her for life. We can make following Jesus the adventure of living with tiptoe expectation about the ways He shows up to teach, comfort, and befriend. We can make His Word the most exciting book available, because something happens when we obey it.

We can change the future. The children we disciple will take their places in a world we won't recognize. We must make discipling our children our daily passion. We must come from fresh encounters with Jesus to invite them to learn along with us. We must send them as a message into the future that will far outlive anything else we could do or say. We must never believe the job is finished, never delegate it to someone else, never take a break from living in ways that encourage children to follow Jesus.

We must never, ever stop discipling.

TIME TO COMMIT

We know what we need to do. Let's just start doing it. Let's make a commitment here and now that we'll eagerly accept God's instruction about raising our children to live with extraordinary faith. Let's take the adventure seriously for ourselves and make every day count. Let's pray more. Let's have more spiritual conversations with our children. Let's admit it when we fall short of God's standards. Let's make sure that no one who lives in our families will ever have to witness hypocrisy. Let's bring everything under the lordship and instruction of Jesus: sports, television, money, vacations, language, entertainment—everything. Let's take the call of Jesus more seriously than ever before. Let's say yes to Jesus and bring a lot of people with us—especially the children.

FOR PARENTS AND MINISTRY WORKERS

1. Take the Disciple-maker's Test, and calculate your score. Choose two statements, and turn them into discipling goals for the next month.

2. Using the questions on page 175, make a plan that includes a prayer time for you, a discipling goal, an activity that will help you accomplish the goal, an evaluation question, and a way for you to be accountable to another person for the plan.

3. Write a prayer committing to the discipling work that Jesus instructs.

4. Download the leader's guide for this book, and consider ways to join with other parents and teachers to study it together.

A DISCIPLE-MAKER'S PRAYER

Eternal God, I'm overwhelmed that you trust me with your children. Your plan for helping them know you through my obedience sends me to my knees. But it's there I hear your call more clearly and offer the only answer I can give—yes, Lord, yes! You lead, and I'll follow—with as many children as you allow me to influence. In the name of the Master Disciple-maker I pray. Amen.

APPENDIX

The following are additional resources you may find helpful as you commit to discipling children.

If Jesus Were a Parent, by Hal Perkins, available at <office@gv-naz.org>. A book by a parent for parents.

Guide to Effectively Training Children, by David Welday, available at <www.nextgeninstitute.com>. A short but pointed summary of what makes a difference in ministry to children. A great resource for ministry workers.

Raising Kids to Extraordinary Faith: 13-week Leader's Guide, is another free downloadable <www.beaconhillbooks.com>.

So . . . Who Is a Disciple-maker? by Lynda Boardman. This pamphlet helps define for children the importance of how to disciple others. Purchase the pamphlet and download the free leader's guide at <www.wordaction.com>.

EXAMPLES OF YOUNG READER BIBLE STORY BOOKS

The Beginner's Bible. Grand Rapids: ZonderKidz Publishing, 2005. More than 90 favorite Bible stories come to life in this collection. *The Beginner's Bible* is the 2006 Retailers Choice Award winner in Children's Nonfiction.

Gilbert Beers. *Early Readers Bible.* Grand Rapids: ZonderKidz Publishing, 2001. A controlled vocabulary introduces no more than five new words with each of the 64 easy-to-read stories.

Mary Manz Simon. *Hear Me Read* series. St. Louis: Concordia Publishing House, 1990—2004. Each book in this series teaches a complete Bible story in 25 words or less. Children develop sight vocabulary as they learn to recognize simple words. Levels 1 and 2 available.

The Phonetic Bible Stories. St. Louis: Concordia Publishing House. This series builds reading confidence and teaches Bible stories by concentrating on phonetic sounds. Each of the 15 books in the series emphasizes a special phonetic sound. Example: *Bleat!* features the long "e" to retell the parable of the lost sheep. For pre-readers and emerging readers.

Heather Gemmen and Mary McNeil. *The Rocket Reader Series.* Colorado Springs: Cook Communications 2003—2004. There are five levels to match beginning reading abilities. Each level focuses on a specific reading skill. Level 1 uses alphabet sounds, while level 2 begins using phonetics and so on. <www.davidccook.com> offers free downloadables that include coloring pages and word flash cards to go with the series.

EXAMPLES OF AUDIO VERSIONS OF THE BIBLE FOR CHILDREN

Eye in the Ear offers stories on CD accompanied by a book. Three volumes of popular Bible stories. Some are available by streaming, using a Flash 7 plug-in and a fast Internet connection. <http://www.eyeintheear.com/#3>

Faith Comes by Hearing shares the audio Bible for illiterate world areas. Offers the New Testament dramatized from the NIV as a free downloadable file. Also check out the Bible Stick, a unique audio device, at <http://www.faithcomesbyhearing.com>.

Little Kids Audio Adventure Bible. Grand Rapids: ZonderKidz Publishing. <www.zondervan.com>. This award-winning audio presentation by children uses the NIRV, which targets children 4-7. It's available in three volumes: Genesis to Proverbs, Ecclesiastes to Malachi, and Matthew to Revelation. Also includes audio questions and application steps.

The Talking-book Store has the *Little Kids Audio Adventure Bible* available as a purchase to download. Perfect for today's technology. <http://www.talking-book-store.com>

EXAMPLES OF BIBLE TRANSLATIONS FOR CHILDREN

The Adventure Bible. Grand Rapids: ZonderKidz Publishing, 2000. This is a *New International Version* for children 8-12. Includes many basic study resources.

The Adventure Bible for Young Readers. Grand Rapids: ZonderKidz Publishing, 2000. This a good example of the *New International Reader's Version* (NIrv). Offers many study resources, including a dictionary and application ideas.

BIBLE STUDY JOURNALS FOR CHILDREN

Art Murphy. *First Things First: A Spiritual Growth Journal for Children.*Orlando: Arrow Ministries, 2008. <www.arrowmin istries.com> This is a spiral-bound journal for older elementary children to record Bible study discoveries.

STEWARDSHIP RESOURCES FOR CHILDREN

<www.generousgiving.org> has great resources for parents, including a list of scriptures you can use with your children and diagnostic questions for parents. Also lists fables, short stories, and other literature that deals with the subject of stewardship.

Larry Gilbert. *God's Special Gifts for Me*. Elkton, Md.: Church Growth Institute. <www.churchgrowth.org> This fun, lively, illustrated pamphlet uses Bible characters to teach children 8-12 about spiritual gifts. Includes lessons, questionnaire, and scoring section in one 16-page booklet.

NOTES

Chapter 2

1. "My Best Friend, Jesus," and free downloadable leader's guide and PowerPoint presentation for parents and ministry workers, available at <www.wordaction.com/mbfj>.

2. "So . . . You Want to Follow Jesus?" and free downloadable leader's guide, available at <www.wordaction.com/go/BBSKIDS>. A helpful follow-up packet of five simple Bible studies for a new believer.

Chapter 3

1. Ibid.

2. Randy Calhoun, "So . . . You Want to be Baptized? and free download-able leader's guide, available at <www.wordaction.com/go/BAPTISM>. For parents and ministry workers.

3. Randy Calhoun, "So . . . You Want to Take Communion?" and free downloadable leader's guide, available at <www.wordaction.com/go/COM-MUNION>. For parents and ministry workers.

4. The Christian Resource Institute gives a good explanation of the Christian Calendar along with other resources for each season at <http://www.crivoice.org/chyear.html>.

Chapter 5

1. Jody Brolsma, ed., *Pray and Play Bible* (Loveland, Colo.: Group Publishing, 1997).

2. *PrayKids*, published by NavPress. Some issues available online at <http://www.navpress.com/landing/praykids/>.

Chapter 6

1. Bonnie Bruno and Carol Reinsma, *Read Together Bible* (Cincinnati, Oh.: Standard Publishing, 2006).

2. *My Bible Book*. Kansas City: WordAction Publishing. 2006.

3. Children's Bible Quizzing, Kansas City, Mo., <www.wordaction.com>, for grades 1 through 6; this six-year Bible study is excellent for homeschool-ing, small groups, and more. Competition enhances the Bible study but is not required.

4. *Connect* is a full-color quarterly magazine filled with ideas for family devotional time and is available at <www.wordaction.com>.

Chapter 7

1. Children's tithing envelopes are available from Nazarene Publishing House at <nph.com>.

2. Tom Felder, "So . . . You Want to Give to God?" available at <www.wordaction.com>.

3. Leader's guide is available at <www.wordaction.com/go/give>.

4. Penny A. Zeller, *77 Ways Your family Can Make a Difference* (Kansas City: Beacon Hill Press of Kansas City, 2008).

Chapter 8

1. Karen Burton Mains, *Making Sunday Special* Nashville: Star Song Communications Group, 1994), <http://mainstay.stores.yahoo.net/makes unspec.html>.

2. See

3. Ibid

4. "My Best Friend, Jesus: Salvation Booklet," available at <www.word action.com>.

5. "So . . . You Want to Share Jesus available at <www.wordaction.com>.

6. Pam Andrews and Barry Robertson, *Splash Kingdom: A Life-saving Musical for Kids*, available from Lillenas Publishing Company at <www .lillenas.com>.

7. "EvangeCube." JESUS Film. Download instructions for presenting the gospel using the EvageCube, or find out how to purchase them, at <http://www.jfhp.org/resources/evangecube/evangecube.html>.

8. "Kids' EE Cube." Kids' EE Ministries. These follow the Kids' Evangelism Explosion approach (see <http://kidsee.org/home.htm>) and are also available through JESUS Film Harvest Partners at <http://www.jfhp.org/resources/evangecube/evangecube.html>.

9. Information on collecting and mailing crisis care kits is available at <http://www.ncm.org/min_ndr.aspx>.

Make a Lasting Difference in Your Child's Life

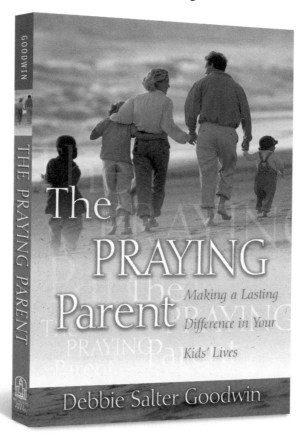

The most important gift you will ever give your child is prayer. This book provides scripture, illustrations, reflection questions, and specific examples to help you learn to pray for your children throughout the moments and stages of their lives.

The Praying Parent
By Debbie Salter Goodwin

ISBN: 978-0-8341-2176-8

Available wherever books are sold.

Help your child live the most independent and fulfilling life possible.

Using her own experience, professional advice, and suggestions from other parents, Debbie Salter Goodwin shows you how to help your child with special needs discover that life empowered by God is never disabled.

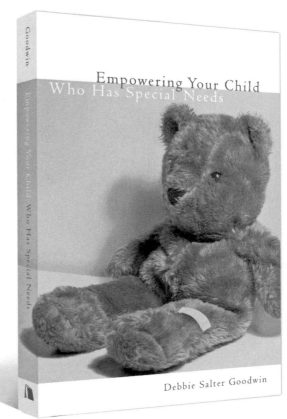

She'll help you:

- Accept realities and make empowering choices within your new boundaries
- Help your child grieve a life of continual losses
- Learn to access and negotiate the medical maze
- Establish prayer principles to help you stay focused on God's resources in difficult circumstances
- Prepare you and your child for the transitions from childhood to adolescence to adulthood

Also from Beacon Hill Press

From financial concerns to passing on macho, *Single Moms Raising Sons* offers honest insight, unifying encouragement, and practical applications to help mothers raise their boys to be the solid, Christian men they want them to be.

Single Moms Raising Sons
Preparing Boys to Be Men When There's No Man Around
By Dana S. Chisholm

ISBN: 978-0-8341-2308-3

Available wherever books are sold.